Table of Contents

INTRODUCTION

We live in an ever-evolving world; nothing ever remains the same. You know, with each passing day, life becomes somewhat more complicated, highly demanding, more daunting, and what have you. And no, it's not just you; it is because we all are gradually easing into that age: the technology age- which of truth has a lot of cons as it does has its pros.

So, there is this issue with your personal growth and development, coupled with clashes and altercations with your family members, a colleague at work, or even a random individual. It is like a new world altogether filled with its own form of challenges and hitches.

But amidst all of these, will there ever be a headway? For you, as an individual, who is probably still young and trying to figure out a lot, will there ever be that spark that just ignites your entire being? Like a mirage lamp lighting up your way and causing just that change you desire in this sweeping world of change. Will you really ever make relevance or some level of impact, at least within your circle? Is there any sort of significant development or personal growth that can emanate from living amidst these rumbles and shifts in today's society? Too many questions!

Truth be told, you can be sure to get a 'yes' to all of these questions because, ideally, the increasing difficulties and challenges we face as individuals make self-growth and personal development even more essential. The reason being that these daunting situations are not only increasing; they are also universal. If we will bear witness of a change to these changes, it has to be based on similarly universal, self-pronounced tenets- such as common to every thriving society throughout the record of history.

Simply put, except you can learn, identify, and implement specific laws or guidelines governing the transformation you seek, then nothing is really ever going to happen. It is also important to note that how we exert these principles differ, and this is because;

i.   It is a universal challenge, and there are several individuals (from a different race, ethnicity, religion, social status, age group, etc.) in the universe;

ii.   Our strengths, gifts, and resources, as individuals, are unique to our person.

iii.   The application of these principles is, therefore, hinged on our individual uniqueness.

It makes it fair to then state that individuality doesn't deter harmony, which, in the real sense, is leverage for all-round success. When you begin to see your personal growth and self-development as compliance for societal change, it will appear that the pressure you will now feel isn't in the negative- as to a feeling of the inability to have achievements to your credit. On the contrary, it is constructive- of wanting to lend a hand in the betterment of your society, our society.

As earlier mentioned, these guidelines constitute adjustments to enable you to see yourself and even the world in a different, more inspiring, and actual sense, and at the same time, improve your behavior and attitude towards achieving the greater good. In the process of exerting these guidelines, you will discover that they are in disparity to the thoughts and practices of today's people. You will begin to see the errors of putting independence over interdependence, making excuses rather than taking responsibility, wanting to purchase or spend more than you save and invest, embracing work over rest, to mention a few. You will also discover the truth in the belief that even the littlest of attempts can make the most impact.

As they say, "you are the change you want to see," and regardless of the tumults and seemingly hostile surroundings, this is possible. Like roses grow among thorns and gold comes out priceless despite the furnace, you too can tell of significant growth and personal development amidst the tides and waves.

As you proceed to read this book, keep in mind your personal needs and challenges, not forgetting those of your association, society, and maximally, the world. In doing so, you are better able to identify and implement lasting guides to help your approach to the situation. You can be sure to have a great adventure as you journey through the writings of the book. Remember to apply every guideline and principle as they are pivotal to the change we so desire. It may seem a daunting task, but these guidelines have allowed for more success, joy, and fulfillment, and in all certainty, yours will be no different.

MINDSET

The first determining factor in achieving your desired outcome has to be the habitual thought pattern, that is, mindset. It is a broad subject. Nevertheless, before understanding the relationship between your mindset and your level of success as an individual, you need to assess your attitude. This is because you will only learn to control life and all of its happenings by first learning to control your mind.

The Human Mind

Beyond just the four-lettered word 'mind,' the human mind is a seat of power. Science reveals that the human mind is a complex assemblage of both cognitive and non-cognitive abilities. It is, therefore, a seat of several senses.

The sense of; imagination, perception, thinking, consciousness, reflection, judgment, memory, and intelligence, all reside in the human mind. Your willpower, instinct, and emotions are also elements of your mind. The expression of feelings and the complexity of decision-making are products of the mind. You literally live in your mind. That is how much of an asset the human mind is.

With your mind, you are more aware of your environment and, therefore, consciously or subconsciously, take information from there, which you process and act upon. Other times, it is just a nudging from the inside of what should be and what ought not to be. These intuitions and information form the basis of our disposition, actions, and pretty much what we now refer to as mindset.

What Is Mindset?

The combination of our beliefs and thoughts, which directly or indirectly affects the way we view; ourselves (first), the immediate environment, and the world at large, is the mindset. Simply put, it is the positioning of your logic, your consciousness, your awareness, your will, and every other component of the human mind. Your mindset is your view, disposition, opinion, or perception of anything at all. Of course, it is a big deal! Your mindset defines your values, your pursuit, your growth, and even your success.

Carol Dweck was absolutely right when she stated that "the best predictor of success in life is your mindset." Remember that this book's success is more personal than it is professional; hence a good tie to the knot is to state that your mindset best predicts your self-growth.

The thing about the mind is that it has a direct impact on your behavior. It influences your quality of life, your sense of fulfillment, and pretty much everything relating to you.

Take an example of two individuals (A and B) who get set for their daily activities; A begins the day with a feeling of appreciation- of self, and an additional opportunity to make life happen. A further goes on to remind himself of who he is by looking into the mirror and saying to the reflected image, "You are amazing, positive and strong-willed. It might not be easy, but you always have, and you still can do it."

B, on the other hand, gets out of bed gloomy, continually fussing about the cumbersome tasks that lie ahead, the difficulty in the chores, and how much of a mess he's got caught up in. "I can't deal with this," B says. "It always ends in the same way. This path definitely wasn't meant for me". "I'm done."

Who, among these two, would you say has greater chances of completing the day's tasks and coming out successfully? In all honesty, A played the mindset game amazingly. Perfectly taking the bull by the horn and coming out even stronger.

That there, briefly captured in a scenario, is the power of mindset. See why it's a big deal?

The mindset is a complex of our ideas, thoughts, beliefs, and attitudes, all of which influence our desires and actions. Understanding each of these concepts is pivotal to revealing the broad framework of the mindset and, subsequently, its effect on self-growth and success.

- **Beliefs**

    Contrary to popular opinion, beliefs are usually not hinged on facts. Often, our individual experiences as we go through life inform our ideas and influence our certainty about a lot of things. Many of the beliefs you hold today, either politically or spiritually, are not based on facts you read or heard. However, because of the authenticity of the experiences shaping those beliefs, you strongly hold on to them.

    For instance, your belief about your intelligence can be based on your experience of it. If you have been able to trump several standards, which are measures for intelligence, you will naturally be certain of your level of intelligence. Your intelligence, therefore, beyond a fact, is now an outcome of your experience(s).

But for convincing shreds of evidence and strong persuasions, alongside a long time frame, beliefs are very difficult to change.

- **Ideas**

Ideas are quite abstract and, as such, tricky to expound. They are like thoughts or a stream of suggestions that occur in the mind, which, when interpreted, constitute a line of action. Ideas don't have to be intentional. Sometimes, thoughts pop up in your mind involuntarily, without you intending this or that. More often than not, our ideas form the basis of our beliefs. With time and experience, your certainty about an idea makes it a conviction.

- **Attitudes**

Your attitude is more or less your immediate temperament towards someone or something. Note the word 'immediate.' It's like your first response to an experience or your first impression of a person or thing. Because attitudes are immediate responses, they are subject to change.

If a new face shows up at your workplace, the chances are that you'll either like or dislike the person. Your attitude of showing like or dislike towards this person will be based on a lot. Many times, if well traced, this attitude is influenced by a premonition- which can still be likened to your mindset. But, with time, as you begin to engage this 'new face' and relate with the person more often, you can be persuaded to have a change of attitude. You can now begin to like a person whom you initially disliked, or vice-versa.

While your mindset about this person determined your attitude towards them, your attitude further strengthened your conviction (mindset) about them.

These concepts are interrelated but form the bedrock of our mindset, and invariably, our accomplishments. Our success or failure as individuals is the first result of our beliefs. These beliefs, alongside our thoughts, influence our attitude and response to personal growth and development, and subsequently, reinforces the positivity or negativity of our mindset. Your mindset goes as far as determining the extent of your mental capacity. It affects you in ways you cannot even measure.

To have a good mindset is to be an inch closer to identifying and wanting to apply the principles guiding the attainment of personal success with respect to self-growth and development. Your mindset is more than just a consistent thought. It is as powerful as allowing you to or hindering you from staying committed to achieving your goals. It is, therefore, essential to position this fundamental element rightly.

What Defines The Mindset?

No one just wakes up to possess a particular mindset. Our mindsets are either decided or influenced. As individuals, several things define our mindset. Recall that the mindset comprises of ideas and beliefs which define individual thought patterns. Simultaneously, these thought patterns influence our feelings, desires, and much more, our actions. While our ideas, beliefs, attitudes, and disposition can be traced to be results of our feelings, thoughts, emotions, and/or desires, a lot of other factors determine our mindset.

Our upbringing, the association we keep, and even the build-up of information and experience from our immediate environment constitute our mindset. By training or observation, we all have learned lessons from those around us, thus defining our outlook.

A quick look at the subject of upbringing reveals that our unique backgrounds, different parents and parenting systems, and even our schooling affect our mindset. Parenting, for instance, involves several styles, systems, and approaches, all of which have their advantages and disadvantages in the ward. Some forms of parenting, like the authoritarian style, have some downsides to a child's mindset. If you happen to have an authoritarian background, there is every possibility that you will battle with issues such as; self-esteem, accepting mistakes, making better choices, anger, tolerance, etc. This is because authoritarian parents seldom discipline their wards; they are strict, enforce rules, and mete out punishment when those rules are broken. Hence, children with such backgrounds grow up constantly feeling sorry for their errors or being bitter and angry altogether. These children are never confident because they feel they are not good enough.

Children from permissive and uninvolved backgrounds also have some defects in their mindset. If your parents or guardians were indulgent and liberal when raising you, or were absent most of the time, then you may find out that you have a problem with growth and development. Growth involves adhering to rules and taking up responsibilities, but for an individual who grew up without rules and had the disposition to do what he wants or deems fit, taking up responsibilities might be an issue. Children of permissive and uninvolved parents also express bad behavioral patterns, which also goes a long way in the way they think.

Please note that these instances of the varying parenting styles that there are isn't to create an impression, nor is it to raise an offense, especially for individuals who are products of the parenting styles mentioned. It is only to affirm as clearly as possible the effects of our background and upbringing on our mindsets as humans.

Other times, not our upbringing, but our association strengthens our ideologies and, at the same time, our mindset. While friends are made to serve as support systems and cheerleaders, especially at lonely times, you may discover that some beliefs your friend(s) hold has rubbed off on you. People with smart and confident friends, even though timid, will sooner or later learn to stand tall regardless. This is because, ideally, your friends are to increase your sense of belonging. You feel accepted by them and vice-versa.

Your mindset is a complex of your thoughts, ideas, beliefs, and attitudes that can be influenced by people, the environment, or even your experience- which always involves your upbringing and social circle. At the end of the day, our background and association are more influential than we imagine. Until we are also actively involved in these structures and how they influence our thoughts, ideas, beliefs, and attitudes, and sometimes make corrections where necessary, we might only remain victims of seemingly supporting structures.

How Is Your Mindset?

The above is a pertinent question and shouldn't be overlooked. How is your mindset? In what manner do you view things? When it comes to self-growth, are you of the opinion that it is valid and achievable? Is your mindset one that dares to do whatever it intends, come what may? Do you think more negative than positive? The response to these questions and more is central to understanding the manner of your perception.

Ideally, as far as self-growth and personal development are concerned, there are two forms of the human mind. There is that which is positioned to see success achieved by diligence, commitment, and growth, and there is another which views success as inborn. Based on the general way of judging a thing as positive and its comparative other as negative, the former mindset (that validates growth) is often taken as the positive side. At the same time, the latter is classified as negative.

It isn't difficult to identify the form of mindset you possess, especially seeing that your pursuit and outcomes are, more often than not, a reflection of your mindset. While the two main forms of mindset will be discussed later in this chapter, let's do a little check on your perception.

Take a quick reversion to your last recorded failure (as an individual). If your perception about that failure is hinged on your incapabilities and you further resolved to do something entirely different (perhaps matching your natural abilities), then you are not so positive about self-growth. However, if you saw the failure as a privilege to stretch yourself, acquire knowledge, learn new skills (to augment your chances of succeeding), then that's positive. You are keen on self-growth and improvement and will do all you can to succeed.

Bear in mind that to have a positive mindset towards self-growth doesn't necessarily mean the belief that an individual can do everything, even when they lack the abilities needed. No! This isn't the 'jack of all trades' mentality. The positive mindset role in self-growth only holds that when your mind is set on a task (or endeavor), even when you lack the natural abilities that define your competence therein, self-development and consistent attempts are enough to set you on course. You might back out of that endeavor at the end of the day, but not because you thought you were 'incapable' and not because you never attempted.

Positive Mindset vs. Negative Mindset

If you grew up being constantly instructed to try new things, take risks, and explore ideas, you are likely to fall into the first category (the positive mindset). This is what Dweck defines as the growth mindset. Individuals in this category strongly believe that talents, skills, and intelligence can be improved upon. It only takes time and, maybe, experience. They, therefore, hold in high esteem the principle of diligence and effort to achieve lasting success (both personally and professionally)—such a beautiful and healthy way of thinking.

On the other hand, if yours is the case of growing into the belief that places little or no value in acquiring knowledge, then you are of the second category (which will be further termed negative mindset). According to Dweck, individuals in this category have a fixed mindset. They believe that success is innate and largely dependent on individual talents and traits, other than diligence and individual effort. They also believe that our distinct traits and qualities as individuals are fixed and cannot be developed, improved, nor changed. In simple terms, the individual with a fixed mindset believes that they already have all they need to succeed and need not bother about self-growth and/or personal development. On the other hand, the individual with a growth mindset can improve their innate abilities seeing that growth is pivotal to success.

To pitch your tent with the fixed mindset category will imply that if you are naturally unintelligent, shabby, and dull, you will remain that way as the belief is that there is really nothing to be done to change your state. Apparently, dwelling on this mindset will suggest that success isn't for all and that except you have been handpicked and blessed by the divine, you cannot boast of success. How demeaning! The issue with the fixed mindset is the belief that "you are not good enough and, as such, cannot thrive in a given endeavor." The growth mindset, however, sees these innate abilities as springboards to success. That is, success can be yours if you are willing and determined to own it. Note that this isn't to portray everyone as similar (just like a fixed mindset will not see everyone as the same). It only implies that although all humans are distinct (in terms of skills and abilities), we all can be better if we attempt to. A little smarter mindset there. Quite positive, even.

Again, for the fixed mindset, success will be based on the standard. That is, except your innate abilities and performance outweigh the laid down standards (in whatever setting, sphere, or institution), you cannot be referred to as successful. There will therefore be limits to the skills and abilities you can exude as an individual as "no man is an island." With limits then comes restriction and deficiency of abilities and, subsequently, a cutback on success. To view success from a growth mindset, however, is to recognize the importance of individual effort in inciting the anticipated achievement. It is to accept that a failure or setback does not define your potential.

Observe that both mindsets are appreciative of success and achievements. However, the distinction between both outlooks lies in their view of the pathway to success and their response to defeat. The fixed mindset, for instance, sees innate qualities (talents and skills) as the ticket to success. The growth mindset, on the other hand, counts diligence, human effort, and development of the 'innate skills,' better ingredients for success.

When it comes to the response of each of these categories to defeat, people with the growth mindset place growth and self-development over negativity and failure. They never agree nor conclude that they are failures simply because they cannot do something. The question for them is, "What is wrong with trying?" After all, a constant attempt could just be all that is required to hit that achievement. The fixed mindset, however, is quick to accept failures and inabilities. To them, there is no need for growth or development if you are inherently unable and incompetent.

Why Do We Turn To Negativity?

Everyone, at a time or the other, has felt the urge to want to give up on self-improvement and success in general. But, to constantly dwell in thoughts of your failures, setbacks, and inabilities, especially without a sense of positivity or determination to make the best of that situation and boast of success, in the end, is wrong. Again, that is the fixed mindset playing out. It is that nudge or feeling that you still can do nothing about your failures.

A couple of factors make the average individual resolve to negative thoughts. A record of continuous failures, low perception of self (with respect to innate qualities), and fear about what the future holds, etc. Negative thoughts could also be the resultant effect of drugs and an unhealthy lifestyle.

While you might want to consider the possibility of having negative thought processes, know this- falling prey to negative thinking is very easy. This is because, many times, it happens involuntarily. Unplanned.

Because our thinking aligns with our feelings, each time we find ourselves in situations or experiences that make us feel bad, our thinking naturally follows that line. The same is the case for experiences that bring about positive feelings.

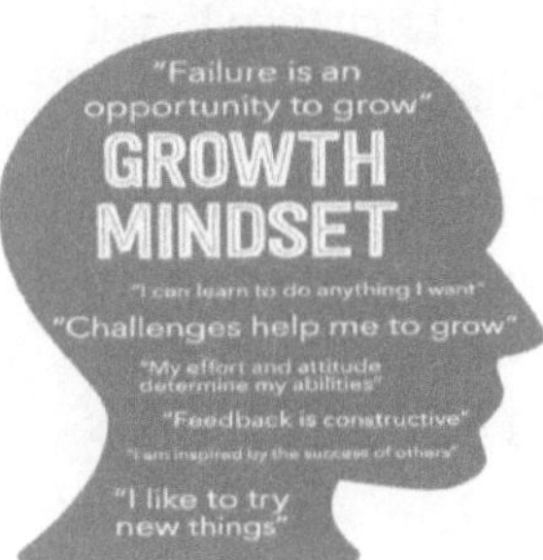

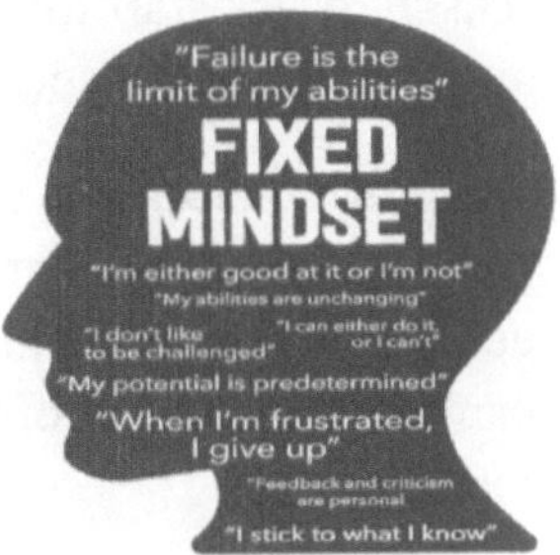

How Can It Hold You Back?

Not many believe that a person's mindset can hinder them from making and/or being the change they so desire. Going back to the two basic forms of mindset earlier discussed in this chapter, viz; Fixed (or negative mindset) and growth (or positive mindset), you will realize the possibility of being held back by your ideas and beliefs.

If you happen to be in the fixed mindset category, every event, set up, or gathering geared towards growth, self-help, personal development, etc., will be considered unnecessary as you are of the mindset that no degree of improvement can heighten your chances of succeeding in an endeavor which you are naturally unfit for, and incapable of. However, for the growth mindset category, even the belief in change and improvement is enough reason to kick-start the journey to change in self and, invariably, the society at large.

The previous scenario of the thought patterns of two individuals- both were preparing to accomplish their laid down goals, further explains the concept of being held back by one's mindset.

While it seemed like A had all it takes to accomplish his goals, all he really had was a positive will. Strong, resilient, and determined. Safe to say that the growth mindset gives just the needed confidence and push to accomplish personal and professional goals. B, on the other hand, could have seemed to also have all it takes to go through the day, but was held back by merely thinking his goals and pretty much the tasks assigned to them, are unachievable. It wasn't a mere thought, after all. His mindset caused the holding back.

At the end of the day, our mindset as individuals is a huge determinant of our bold tendencies. A negative mindset is the first obstacle to growth and development, regardless of the sphere. The negativity is thus seen in your inability to grow your skills, augment your chances, and further pursue what you initially desired.

Turning from negative to positive thinking

As mentioned earlier, everyone (at least occasionally) feels the pressure to yield to negative thinking. However, the positivity we express is based on our ability to deal with these negative thoughts. That is, while negative thoughts (as it relates to the fixed mindset) can involuntarily spam the mind, you can either accept or reject these negative thoughts and, in the long run, be in control of your mindset.

Contrary to what you think, switching from a fixed (or negative) mindset to a growth (positive) mindset is possible. Great news, after all. The process might seem a little complex or befuddling, especially because your present mindset results from ideas, beliefs, experiences, and even your upbringing- all of which have accumulated over time. Other times, in the process of changing your perception to a more willing yet determined one, you could even pause to ascertain that you're not losing your mind or something in that direction. It is very understandable.

But, know this, turning from negative to positive thinking is not only favorable; it is also viable. The level of effectiveness that stems from having positive thought patterns is enough to stir anyone who will inherently (or so it seems) think lowly or undesirably. There are three stages to the switch. Call it the ABC step to positive thinking.

A- Acknowledge

Acknowledge that you're at a fix. If you have been reading all along and have spotted that you have some thought patterns corresponding to those of the fixed mindset, it's good you recognized. Acknowledgment is the beginner step to a switch. Except you come to the level of recognizing your negative mindset tendencies and much more accepting the ill in them, there isn't much to be done.

Acknowledgment wouldn't come from a place of regret and bitterness. Rather, it is to consent that this is where you are and to admit you need a change. Note that it is one thing to recognize your shortcoming, and it is another thing to be willing to change the mindset. Both are necessary for this stage. Do not just recognize your wrong beliefs and views to personal growth and success but also come to a position seeking to switch.

B- Believe

Just as stated earlier, it might take time and a lot of funny experiences, but the switch from negative thinking to a more positive one is ideal and very possible. Like anyone will naturally heal from a break-up or get over a deceased friend (or relative), you too can "get rid of or get over" whatever fixed yet negative mindset you've always possessed. It only requires time, your willingness, and a little bit of patience. You'll also be needing all the support you can get, and just, so you know, this book is all of that and more. Recognized the ill in your mindset? Acknowledged and believed you need to switch. Good! Come on board!

C- Correct

Having seen and embraced the possibility of switching from a negative mindset to a much positive one, you can now take the bold step of correcting these beliefs. The correction will include a 'disbelief' of the previous views and opinions and then replace these previous thought patterns with even new, Growth stimulating thought patterns.

How to Think Positively

Our thoughts and beliefs as individuals are interwoven. At the same time, both constitute our actions and inactions as it pertains to self-growth and development. Seeing that both our thoughts and beliefs form the basis of our mindset as individuals, our general attitude to life and all it entails, it is thus needful to learn the process of having a strong yet positive mindset as well as the long term benefits of having such.

It should be noted that the 'how' to this is beyond steps or guidelines to simply adhere to. It involves the life patterns pivotal to long term personal (and professional) success and should be seen in that regard. In thinking positively, and subsequently, to build a growth mindset, each of these beliefs is important:

- **Learning is without limits**

    If you have always thought that there is an extent to the knowledge you can acquire, you'll have to make some adjustments to that. While this isn't to mean that you should know a thing about everything (as you must have heard before now), acquiring knowledge- new or more- about anything at all hurts no one. What's more to life but to learn and keep learning? The individual who puts a halt to learning has a great problem handling growth, and that is because, to a large extent, growth is hinged on knowledge. Have the mindset that treasures learning. It is a beautiful one.

Another side to this will be to be mindful of the belief that you can grow or achieve lasting success by 'doing what you know how to do best,' even if it's just one thing. For one, to think that way is to be manipulative. On second thought, it is demeaning. Why deprive yourself of the benefits of learning anew? Yes, benefits. To continually learn is to stay informed, engaged, and inspired to thrive. To think that there is this level of confidence and self-appraisal that emanates from your bank of knowledge. Why not? Be open to learning. Never despise knowledge. Seize the time, take the opportunity, and learn regardless. It is never too late or needless to learn. In doing so, you will come across platforms and opportunities instrumental to your growth and development.

Know this, the mindset that seeks to learn will thrive in trials and challenges because its intention/focus is to learn a thing or more from whatever situation of life.

- **Challenges are propellants**

This might not look like it but believe it is so. When you have this view about challenges, you will be open to them. For one, seeing challenges as propellants helps you make a good preparation for whatever challenge that may come your way as against the upset you express when you face one. However, there is an extreme to this mindset- this will be the thought pattern positioned to always expect a challenge in every endeavor—a very tricky one there. Relax.

This is not to say that challenges will not come your way; neither is to imply that you must (emphasis on must) experience a challenge in every endeavor. No. The balance of this mindset is to utterly welcome challenges. If they come, great. Take them as stepping stones to excellence. Suppose they do not, great still.

Again, the mindset that accepts challenges and setbacks is not a facade or a covering for failure. Today, it is believed by many that people who are somewhat welcome to challenges are 'failures' who never get the hang of their pursuit and then hide under cover of 'always expect setbacks.' To think this way will be false. The openness to challenges is simply not to throw you off balance should challenges really come your way. It's that simple.

So, accept challenges. Many successful persons today are products of one challenge or the other, and when asked about the experience, the summary is they all got stronger and better through each hurdle. It makes it seem like challenges further full us with the belief that we can do more than we actually thought.

You see, the mindset that welcomes challenges is one that learns bravery and dares to take risks, and that of truth is instrumental to the pursuit of growth and development. What then? Thrive through challenges. Dare to take risks. Only ensure that they are contributory to your personal pursuits and seek to grow in the process.

- **I can ask for help**

Having this mindset, just having learned to be daring in the face of challenges, is no mistake. So, you are set to take the bull by the horn. In your words, "There is no turning back," "I can do this," "It seems difficult, but I'll pull through," "I'm determined to go through this, regardless." Good! But are you enough for yourself? Have you checked if you do not require a spur? You know, like that ray of sunshine that brightens up the stain on that white apparel.

A fallacy to the courageous mindset is that you really don't need help. Think it through, all through different life stages; we have needed a hand or two to accompany us as we journey through life. That witty friend that comes to your rescue on days when you seem at a fix. Daddy's constant call to be sure you are doing just fine. Pretty old grandma's tales that lift you up in your dark moments. And oh, not to forget mama's fingers gently stroking your hair as you cried it out in her arms. That's life! Co-existence, isn't it? We all are needful of the other

Is this to demean independence? No way! What's growth without sovereignty? But, do not get caught up in the deception that you can do it all by yourself while in pursuit of growth. Yes, we're discussing personal growth, but a little bit of interdependence could double up your outcome. Hence, seek help. Check around (within and without your circle), is there a helpful hand? It could be someone more informed or even more experienced. It makes it better if this 'someone' is willing to offer you help. Never see yourself as too big to request for help, nor as too small to need help. A hand of help will always be to your benefit, so take it. It's a lift to the height you envision. This will further suggest that you pay attention to those you keep in your circle. If they are visionary, success-minded, goal-oriented, determined minds, you can be sure to get the help you need.

- **Always persevere**

People with lasting (personal or professional) success are usually of the 'never give up' opinion. There is no individual with such striking achievements that pulls out just easily. No way! It's team strong all the way.

Perseverance has to be the price for excellence, regardless of the sphere. Those who give up or pull out just at the start of the game never really get the hang of it and cannot tell how pleasurable or repulsive of an experience it was. Do not be that quitter. It doesn't pay off.

Position your thoughts to embrace the art of thriving, regardless. A positive mindset is one that erases the language of giving up. Now, this isn't to mean that your talents or innate abilities are reason enough to keep you going. To have that mentality will be a setback as there is a good number of highly skilled yet personally unsuccessful individuals in society today. Are the skills needed? Of course, yes. Do they guarantee success? Certainly not. What's the point here? Your skills and abilities are not enough. In fact, they are not the yardstick for growth. If you rank best in any field and stay lazy or somewhat unbothered, it's sad, but you'll go nowhere.

Only the inspired, who by all means are ready to put in the work, get through the tough times easier. Without perseverance and strong will, the best at it is only a novice in the game. If you grow in person, you should be determined, strong-willed and perseverant. There should never be 'never' in your thoughts and speech.

- **Today's input is seen in tomorrow's outcome**

Late Zig Ziglar said, "It is your attitude, not your aptitude that will determine your altitude." Amazing how this statement briefly summarises the point. Talent and skill are good; hard work makes things even better. It's saddening to always refer to unsuccessful talents, but it's the best example to drive home the point sometimes. The focus here, beyond perseverance, is the attempt. Do something. Don't just sit doing nothing. Growth is a process, remember? Your hard work and attempt are involved in the process. It's fine to call it labor because, yes, growth is no joke.

So, it is not enough to have the 'never give up' attitude. Channel that attitude into the work you put in. Let's be reminded that our innate abilities as individuals can only take us so far. Our input, coupled with perseverance (earlier discussed), defines the difference in tomorrow's outcome.

It's like an A student thinking residual knowledge is enough to pass an exam. While his residual knowledge can only take him so far, an average student who took the time to prepare upfront will come out better in that examination than the supposed A student. The reason being that the A student relied on his abilities, intelligence, and previous knowledge and failed to put in the effort required in passing the examination.

You don't have to take the path of the A student, relying on your skills and abilities. Gear up for the change you desire. Look away from your intelligence and, maybe, previous accomplishments. Develop a passion for diligence. Work on the character. Be willing to make a difference through your efforts. Do these, as often as you can, constantly and again, and see yourself fly. Fly so high- as high as you so much desire, because you sought to put in the work.

- **It's okay to make mistakes**

It might sound odd, but know that sometimes, you'll make mistakes. It's only the truth. Mistakes don't kill; they only correct or inform. So why not? Agreed, there might be prices to pay, but it doesn't deter you from being successful again. Now, this mindset looks very similar to accepting challenges, but there is a bit of difference. To accept challenges is to be prepared for something that is, many times, beyond you. For mistakes, it is your defect- at least the most part of it- and as such, you are expected to take responsibility. What this mindset of accepting mistakes helps you achieve is efficiency. So, you made a mistake; rather than beat yourself up about it and being wasteful with the time and resources at your disposal, keep at it. There was a mistake, yes. Was it your fault? Yes. You have taken the blame. The larger part of taking responsibility is to make corrections and make it work. You shouldn't dwell on your errors, thereby being wasteful of the passing time and resources. Pick up from you left and make it work. It's okay to make mistakes. The acceptance there is to receive correction from the mistake, avoid another mistake, and move on.

It is imperative to state that with mistakes comes a bit of character check. Look closely; each time you beat yourself up about an error you committed or a friend committed, there is hardly a nudge to forgive. And that's because either filled with guilt, hurt, or anger. These feelings are detrimental to personal growth. Anyone battling feelings of anger and guilt hardly want to try again. And if there's no trying, sadly, there's no development. You see, all that negativity attached to a little error committed in such a short while. Hence, the need to position your mind to accept mistakes- committed by you or someone else. There is no harm in mistakes. If anything, you pay the price, and the price again is for your betterment. See that. With mistakes comes a level of experience, maturity, knowledge, adaptation, efficiency, and opportunity to do it right. That's a success, and it is, lasting.

A quick address to those individuals who embark on every endeavor with the opinion to always make mistakes. If you are of that school of thought, it is extreme. You may never grow from that because somewhere in your mind, mistakes are more of a routine than an opportunity. Watch it. You do not always have to make mistakes, but when you do make one, don't be filled with regrets. Forgive yourself (or whoever committed the error) and be resilient. That's much better.

- **Don't stop improving**

Just as you have seen that learning is without limits, improving is a drive to your aptitude. Reciting lines such as "I can always improve" to yourself every morning is enough to set you on course. It's like reminding yourself that the skills and abilities you presently possess are not enough and that there is more to what you can actually do. Be on the lookout; are there upgrades to the skills you possess? Go for it. What this thought pattern does is that it strengthens your relevance. Don't be that traditional artisan who lives down the street. Improve! You shouldn't think you have it all planned at every point in time.

Review your plans. There might be a line of action missing or one requiring advancement. If you have only desired personal growth for yourself and not as a basis for impact and change in your society, then it's got to change. This thought patterns us for improvement, and your goals are no exception. Improve your goals as much as you seek to improve in the process that helps you achieve them. Improvement is not impossible. It only requires a drive, and the mindset to always want to improve is the initial drive. The next thing is to be observant and aware. Be aware of the changes around you- changes in skills, ideas, technology, etc. Observe them. As you observe, be willing to stretch yourself to take up these changes for your betterment. Then, progress. Progress in doing that which you intend- improve!

That's it! Somewhat extensive, but very helpful.

Now, unlike you already think, these beliefs are not going to permanently fill your constant thought patterns (just like that). There will be conflicts, maybe sometimes. Somewhere in your mind, you will feel the persuasion to think otherwise, to want to put yourself in a mix of both the fixed and growth thought patterns. This contrast will often occur, especially within this stage of wanting to birth new beliefs and with the presence of individuals with several conflicting mindsets around you. But it's fine. You can always work around such an experience.

To start with, each time you feel the rise of a conflicting thought pattern, shun it with a reminder of the new belief systems. You might need to say the positive words out clearly; other times, a reminder within does the trick.

Whichever way, never lose grasp of your new beliefs (as it pertains to self-growth). Sooner or later, these beliefs will serve as a build-up for a growth mindset. They will thus trigger accomplishments based on self-development and positive thinking other than that which is solely based on innate abilities.

On a final note, self-growth is all about pioneering the change we desire in our society and the world. To take up that step requires a lot- the first of which is to change your mindset. When you succeed at imbibing a mindset that is similar to and supportive of your goals and aspirations, there will be no holding back to success- personally and globally.

PERSPECTIVE

"The eye sees only what the mind is prepared to comprehend"- Robertson Davies.

Still on this self-examination journey is the need to understand the concept of perspective and all that exists. Very similar to your mindset is your perspective; it tells of your view or outlook on many things. However, while mindset is more of a pattern of thinking and a disposition towards achieving goals and targets, perspective defines the understanding or judgment of one's environment. It is the ability to observe things in a way different from others. Let's just say mindset is the tabletop upon which other experiences and judgments like perspective are built. It pretty much explains the importance of perspective. It is that mental perception peculiar to an individual without which even a growth mindset appears to be fixed.

Consider the image below; it is a good illustration of the different perspectives there can be to even the littlest of issues. Yet, all of these perspectives possess a level of validity. A complete view of whatever situation the image is made to represent is to pay attention to all the different sides to it.

Life is a mystery, and it unfolds in diverse ways. As an individual, you really cannot get the hang of the different sides of life. There will always be a limit to your view about any situation or subject. This is not to sound offensive; our limited experiences account for the difference in our perspective concerning anything at all. Hence, the need to always accept the holistic approach to a situation.

Bringing this down to our day-to-day lives filled with diverse experiences for each of us as individuals, is it not possible that the perspective you hold as true (in any situation at all) is dissimilar to what another holds as true in the same situation? Regardless of how we choose to view the scenario, is it not reasonable that a perspective other than yours can still be true? Although there may be clear and general views on certain issues- marriage, growth, gender roles, and responsibilities, etc., if closely observed, each of us still holds varying views on these issues.

See another image below.

In the image, the guy on the left-hand side can only see a six. Regardless of what the issue is or what other dimensions there can be to the ground, he is right. The guy on the right-hand side, however, perceives a 9. By all means, from his own point of view, he is also right. To hold both perspectives of the matter is appropriate. The problem with perspective will now be the argument that your own view of the matter is the absolute truth or the only side to the situation. Back to the image, if each of the guys fails to view things from the other's perspective, then there will never be the truth; neither will there be progress. They will only dwell on conflicts for the longest of time.

And that just explains the bulk of the problem we experience in our everyday life. Your disapproval of the validity of another's perspective on yours is the conflict we endlessly try to resolve. The concept of a holistic view is such that it allows us to have a better understanding of a situation and the many sides/perspectives there are to it.

Many times, as individuals, we are held back by not just our mindset to self-growth and its importance in achieving lasting success, but much more by the perspective of our view of what is true. What is needed sometimes is a stepping back to allow us better positioned to view the situation in the best light. Your truth may not always be the truth. Liaising, acceptance, learning are all instrumental to growth, which in the long run, leads to success. Arguments and conflicts are no good base for self-development. Life has made us all different yet unique; Man and woman, young and old, parent and child, leader and follower, we all stand in different positions and are therefore expected to view things differently. Our perspective can either be right or wrong. The validity or falseness of your perspective is not the determinant of another's perspective (which could also be right or wrong, by the way). You could hold opposing views with another, yet you both are right about the scenario.

Unlike you will begin to think, your perspective goes way beyond your physical observation or interpretation of an issue. More than a physical observation, your perspective involves your mental prospect, your thoughts' condition, and your ability to hold significant interrelationships. That is, your perspective is not only a revealing of how you see things but also how you see people, as well as your ability to connect to their relative differences. Your perspective, like your mindset, is dependent on your experience, culture, and even your background (or upbringing).

Perspective involves comparison, imagination, visualizing, reasoning, creation, and manipulation, all of which are instrumental to growth and success. Our perception of a thing is not always the same for another. Hence, the need to be open-minded and receptive to the perspective of others.

What Is The Importance Of Perspective?

One look at this perspective will generate a question, "Why the need to understand perspectives, though?" Perhaps we should start by stating that our perspectives have a huge effect on our individual beliefs and understanding of a subject. In the end, it is slightly interwoven with the mindset theory.

Our perspectives also affect our approach to life. A right perspective, for instance, implies an improved approach to life and all therein, improved interaction with people (regardless of their differences), and, subsequently, an implementation of the expected change in our personal lives and respective communities.

Sometimes, seeing things from another person's point of view helps us to understand them, how they think, and why they do what they do. By so doing, the act of making preconceived judgments about anyone at all is checked. It also unleashes us to a pathway of tolerance and understanding.

Perspective can also be a choice, seeing that you can choose to see things in this way other than the other way. Your decision to be perceived in the way in which you have may or may not have been influenced is entirely your choice anyway. This choice of yours will further determine how you do things or your response to things. Hence, if it was an influenced choice, it could steam regrets. It is, therefore, essential to learning to choose our perspective to avoid being influenced into viewing things and much more responding to them in a certain way.

Perspective is required in almost every sphere, as a student, a researcher, a leader, a follower, and even personal activities. Also, perspective teaches us to validate the authenticity of information before accepting it, rather than concluding or holding on to a particular truth, which might result in altercations, prejudice, and a judgment of people's views, always subject news and information to confirm. Doing this is a caution to avoid friction in our human relationships.

Perspective really does matter- to you as an individual and also to those around you.

The Perspective of a Leader

In our different spheres, we hope to lead even without being the lead. Leadership isn't in position or title but in function and responsibility. A leader is one who stimulates confidence in another and swings them to action. He expresses the ability to influence and guide while still gaining the support of others in the achievement of a mutual task. The crowd looks up to the leader, who directly or indirectly tells them what next to do. A good leader has a growth mindset and always views things holistically because he is conscious of the different people surrounding him.

Learning to perceive things like a leader is pretty much what we need to get rid of conflicts in our everyday life. Much more than helping to reduce conflicts, the leader's perspective; helps to strengthen the growth mindset, reinforces the importance of self-development, and helps in the achievement of enduring success. To have the perspective of a leader is to;

- **Be clear on the idea of 'control.'**

    In developing a leader's perspective, it is first important to be clear on what you can and cannot control. You see, leaders inherently want to assume authority or play the 'I'm in control here' card. Sadly, it doesn't always work this way. Remember, the aim is to learn to accept other perspectives as it is central to improving oneself and much more speeds up the change we desire.

Rushing to take control wouldn't help. Instead of rushing to assume authority or certainty, be patient to recognize what you can influence. You may not directly influence the thoughts or views of people around you, but you can always control your own thoughts, actions, and reactions. With this understanding, you can be patient enough to accept others and their different perspectives related to a progression on the issue at hand.

- **Shun negativity**

Recall that just like your mindset, your perspective influences your response and attitude. To take up a leader's mind in a conflicting scenario is to decide to shun negativity (both in your actions and inactions). When you approach a situation upfront with the mind that shuns negativity, sooner or later, the odds will be in your favor. You will therefore avoid conflicts, hear others out, and make progress in the situation.

- **Always listen**

  Leaders have to be good listeners. As much as you hold a perspective separate from the rest of the crowd, seek to listen. Get the facts from them. Remember that even though the perspective you hold may be true, it doesn't deter the validity of others' perspectives. Listening helps you get the hang of the situation from a different perspective. So, again, be patient enough to listen.

- **Be open to learning**

  It might sound strange, but a leader should also be receptive to learning from the crowd. While learning always involves listening, listening might not always imply learning. Do not just seek to get the facts from the people surrounding you; also endeavor to learn from their perspective. They, too, might be right, after all. The situation can be one involving many perspectives, all of which are valid. So, why hold on to just one of the good perspectives when there is an opportunity to learn more and make the most of the situation.

Success sometimes involves a holistic approach that cannot be achieved without learning from those around you.

- **Think ahead**

As you should already know, leaders think too. Sometimes, way ahead of the crowd. This isn't to mean that the leader is always smarter or more clever than the crowd, but because the leader holds a consciousness of others' interests, he thinks of results best favorable to everyone. In a conflicting situation, while you listen and seek to learn from the perspectives of others around you, take the time to think through. For one, think of your response to the varying perspectives put before you. As you think of the best response, you are indirectly preparing your mind to accept the view that best supports success in the current scenario.

- **Place possibility over fear**

  It is normal to express fear and anxiety in conflicting environments; however, a leader takes the bravery to choose possibility over fear. The conflicts and arguments concerning a situation you are involved in can put even the most courageous of persons on the spot. But rather than expressing fear, you can make the most of the situation from a leader's perspective. This will imply an immediate reflection on what can result from the underlying situation. Instead of being anxious to restore an optimal environment (which will most likely involve the imposition of a perspective), reflect on the possibilities that can arise from the varying perspectives.

- **Be able to manage emotions**

  There is no guarantee that your emotions will always lead you to take the right course of action. What emotions do is to spur you to react based on how you feel and what you desire. Doing this amid conflicting perspectives might seem like an imposition of your perspective- which is like adding fuel to the fire. Instead, defer emotions and express empathy- which is by far better quality. Empathy isn't self-seeking. It often denies self and puts into consideration what the other party will do. Not our ability to share our feelings and emotions, but our competence to regulate our emotions is a requisite for perspective tolerance. Leaders who express empathy are known to have increased influence. At the end of the day, the entire situation seems to be in your favor, whereas all you did was ensure everyone's interest is well expressed.

Although conflicting situations seem difficult, a closer look reveals that there is always an opportunity. We are just always busy trying to make our perspective heard that we often neglect the opportunity to make good use of the situation to record success. Self-improvement is also seen in the ability to recognize the opportunity in the darkest of scenarios and make the best of it, to our advantage, and for the good of everyone around us. This ability (to recognize opportunities, regardless) is enclosed in your perspective.   With the right perspective, regardless of the heat and discomfort at the moment, any individual can soar and possibly lift others too.

Bear in mind that the headway to the concept of perspective isn't to always want to have your way or to always look out for conflicting scenarios. The matter of perspective deals with learning to understand that the world consists of several individuals with unique and varying perspectives. While we all strive to grow personally, the need for interdependence cannot be displaced. As we co-exist and co-depend on one another for personal growth and, subsequently, a universal change, we will run into situations requiring our perspectives.

This concept of perspective, therefore, helps to strengthen our co-existence and co-dependence as individuals and much more hellos to promote our growth and success personally, professionally, and communally.

The Participant's Perspective

Sometimes, having the leader's perspective isn't enough, especially because the goal is to have a holistic view of a situation. Taking the leader's position might not be ideal for every situation. There will be situations requiring your humility, submission, and ability to let go for the greater good. And that is who a participant is. A participant is not necessarily a follower. More than an adherer, a participant is one who is actively involved in a cause.

As important as a leader is to his followers or team members, so is a participant important in a gathering without which the facilitator is only like an empty barrel. The role of participants in any gathering is usually admirable. Contrary to popular opinion, participants are not incapacitated and dependent individuals. Instead, they are individuals who understand the importance of harmony in achieving success. They, therefore, do all they can to ensure they are in unison with other participants as well as the supposed team lead. Not only do we need people with the leader's perspective to make growth possible, but we also need people with the perspective of a participant. This will further balance out the flaws in a conflicting scenario.

As a participant in a conflicting scenario, it is expected that you;

- **Respect differing opinions**

  Variety is the spice of life. We all are unique in-person and, similarly, unique in our thoughts, opinions, and views about any subject at all. Until you come to terms with this fact, you will find it hard to respect differences. Your respect for differences necessarily doesn't mean neglecting your own belief or ideologies; it simply portrays your maturity and readiness to work alongside unique yet distinct personalities. Simply put, your adaptability. Except you learn to respect differing opinions, you will always come off as the frustrated participant. This is because you will always strive to be heard other than to also hear. You will also be blind to the possibilities present in the opinions of other participants.

Furthermore, to learn to respect differences is to be of the 'way out' or 'way forward' mentality. This is because disrespect to individual opinions is scheming for a division. As you take to respect opinions varying from yours, you learn the art of tolerance, which is central to self-improvement.

- **Communicate effectively**

There is no better way to express your perspective on a situation than to communicate it. Perhaps it is important to state that conflicting situations do not just arise because the individuals involved want a conflict. The conflicting scenarios are so because there is a need to agree on an issue, and the agreement will further pave the way for our individual growth and our common success. Hence, the need to express your perspective fearlessly and without ego.

By communicating your perspective, you express your interest and participation in the underlying situation. You expand your mind and reveal a side to your thought patterns. As you communicate your view, seek to either moderate or adjust your perspective. This will help in the progression of a conflicting scenario.

- **Learn to let go**

Unlike you have grown to know, letting go doesn't always portray weakness or acceptance of defeat. Neither does letting go imply ego. No! There are strength and humility in letting go. There will be times that your perspective about a situation will not be picked or accepted by other participants, and that's okay. Recall that your perspective is only aside from the situation. While your perspective may be right, there will still be several right perspectives different from your own. Rather than being bitter that your perspective wasn't chosen, you should be concerned about the viability of the perspective(s) that will be concluded as the truth about the situation. Again, to let go is to be tolerant of other people of their views, which is an essential factor in making the best outcomes of several situations.

- **Be supportive**

If nothing else, a participant is always supportive. To show support is to first be actively involved in a course. In a conflicting scenario, don't be a passive participant. While you might hold on to a perspective (which is either true or not), do not back out of the situation because your perspective seems to be disapproved or disannulled. Remember, togetherness is the bedrock of success. If you can let go, you can show support. Support is expressed in your acceptance of the views of others and, subsequently, in the conclusion of the scenario. With your support, conflict is better fixed, and on time too.

- **Ask questions**

    Sometimes, clarification might be all that is needed to make headway. If, as a participant in the scenario, you are engrossed trying to air your views as much as others are similarly enforcing theirs, you'll be blind to recognize a way out. Don't just stare at others; ask questions. Get clear on the situation. Why is this person's perspective this way? "Am I missing something?" "Where do we go from here?" etc., are some of the questions you can put forward to fellow participants to make light of the situation.

While there may be the incredible feeling of people holding viewpoints different from yours and taking with less significance those things that matter to you, the way to achieve success in such a relationship is by learning to understand and respect their rights to their perspectives. When next you run into a seemingly conflicting situation (with many sides to it), do not just be quick to hold on to the more emphatic perspective; always recall the need to take the holistic view. It helps to improve self and, in the end, results in lasting success. Again, significant victory is only achievable with several selfless minds, each driven by a sense of respect for the others and the mutual benefit resulting from the process.

TAKE CONTROL

In trying to adjust to our consistently awakening world, many of us go through life like we are subject to it. Like we've totally lost control of what to do, what not to do, what happens to us, and, subsequently, how we affect our world. Our dreams and aspirations stare at us in the face as we journey through the path of fear- of our inabilities, our chances of survival, and other things encompassed in the feeling of 'UNCERTAINTY.'

No longer do we dictate our actions. Instead, our actions are reflections of our obligations and anxieties. It all seems like life in its entirety is revolving at such a swift pace, and we can't seem to adapt to the different events it throws at us. Like we are stuck, and there is no way out. The goals we've set seem so far; we cannot reach them. Other times, it's like we are just blinded by all of life's miseries. Like joy and fulfillment were only reserved for some set of persons. Life, rather than happening by us or in our favor, happens to us. We no longer live; we just stay in existence, curled up in worry, as we watch each passing day embittered about our inabilities to do the things we really desire. We practically lose ourselves.

This shouldn't be the case, anyway. Regardless of the hurdles and demands of life, we can always take control of our anxieties and, subsequently, over the happenings of life. Though the obstacles are largely external factors, you can prevent these occurrences from holding you back in achieving your dreams. Just like you feel you have lost control, you can also take back control. You can pull through all the circumstances pulling at you. Within all of these, it is still possible to find a balance- emotionally and physically, think it through, and be your own advocator for change. You can own your life and dictate what and what is not pertaining to the attainment of your goals. You only need to learn and understand the pathway to self-management (or self-control), and with that, you, too, can feel in control of your life.

Self-management

The principle of self-management begins with your choice of wanting to exert control over your life and the happenings around you. Until you really decide to bring the circumstances to a halt, you will only be a dreamer whose wishes are filled with things he still cannot set to do. Till you resolve to take the position of running how things are done in this domain called 'you,' all your desires are but wishes. The truth is, every day, you have the opportunity to make that decision. Much more than the opportunity is your ability to choose to control life (as it pertains to you) or to be controlled by it.

Know that to take control of your life is to practice the leadership of self. It is to take responsibility for yourself and every sphere of your life. Your career, your finance, your health, your happiness, and relationships are the individual spheres contained in your life, which you are now set to lead. This form of leadership further involves the ability to keep negativity in check as you journey through life's multiple challenges, and much more the ability to influence your perception, confidence, actions, and inactions

There should also be a caution to what you let into your mind. Yes, we're back at it again- the mind. That's because we are pretty much what we make of our minds. Our living as humans is largely dependent on our minds. When you lack control over what your mind feeds on, you're nigh on losing your mental focus.

In self-management is; the consciousness to be your own boss, the ability to take responsibility for your actions and inactions (as against playing the victim game), the decision to organize yourself, and put forth ideas and suggestions to your project of self-development.

Being your own boss is the need to do things, carry out tasks without being told by anyone what to do or how to do it. Remember, you are the boss, and you run the show here. It is ideal that you take the vigor to decide what needs to be done, when it should be done and how it should be done. This usually involves a lot of thinking (of course, for yourself) and ultimately taking action. Notice the stress on taking action. Many times, we have no problem with doing the thinking and trying to figure things out, and this is because humans are thinkers. Our emotions, desires, actions, attitudes are all tied to our thinking. It sometimes becomes difficult to decipher if these emotions and attitudes are the results of our thinking or if our thinking results from how we feel and the responses we give. In our conscious and subconscious, we are more often than not thinking. To think for humans is more of a reflex than it is a voluntary action. It is fairly, the reflex nature of the mind. We cannot but think as humans because we are constantly faced with the urgency of making decisions, which is impossible without good thinking. However, while we sometimes come out well in the thinking test, not many proceed to take action, and even when we do, it is, more often than not, a flaw. This issue of not taking actions at all, taking the wrong actions, or inappropriately taking the right actions, constitutes the challenges we face in our personal lives and our human relationships. Just as earlier constructed, our actions (right or wrong) are outcomes of our thinking.

Hence the need to stress the place of doing much yet ideal thinking alongside timely and significant actions is instrumental to the principle of self-management. In thinking and acting rightly, there is the need for drive, belief in self, and resilience because, in self-management, no one tells you what to do. As an institution's boss, you use your initiative to determine what to do and problems to be solved with little or no assistance. While this may seem like you trivializing the essence of collaboration, understand that collaboration does not rule out independence. Your personal growth is directly hinged on your ability to take the lead and secondarily on co-dependence.

The organization is yet another essential skill in the journey of being your own boss. Have you ever seen a leader who is here and there with no strategic layout of the job description of each of the individuals that make up his team? Being disorganized hasn't helped anyone and wouldn't start at this age. A person with an arranged closet gets ready in a shorter time than an individual who has his clothing items all over the place. So, in this self-control journey, it isn't enough to have the initiative and ability to take the right actions; there is also the need to be able to plan your time and activities. As the boss of you, you should be accustomed to identifying those things of urgency and importance (as in the words of Stephen Covey- American author and educator). Asides from managing your time and planning your activities, you should also learn to be prepared for unforeseen contingencies. Certain tools (physical and abstract) are required in carrying out the activities you earlier planned; your ability to get these tools ready and available beforehand is evidence of your organization and a requisite of self-leadership and control.

In self-management, there is no place for blame and victimization. Funnily, we are all so used to playing the victim. To be your own boss is to forgo the days when you willfully or maybe, accidentally make excuses for problems and failures. Enough of "if only's" and more of being accountable. Own responsibility for every result (positive or not). That's what self-management demands. It strengthens efficiency, effectiveness, and productivity.

Sometimes, our ability to properly manage our plans, time, and ultimately ourselves are only a reflection of how much we care for and appreciate yourself. If you mean that much to yourself, then you should be ready to learn, understand, and apply the principle of self-management.

It Starts With You

Understanding the need for self-management is of immense importance in the journey of learning to take control. Like the usual saying, "When the purpose of a thing is unknown, abuse is inevitable," a lack of understanding of the need for control makes the concept of self-control altogether unnecessary or even misused.

For starters, it is only usual and somewhat essential to want to assume control over self. The essence in the feeling of control is more perceived as an adaptation to survival. See it this way, when you are aware of your ability to achieve just your desired results, you will have a better drive to face challenges, no matter how sturdy. More than fueling passion and drive, the perception of control over self also influences the achievement of dreams and attaining goals. Going further, there is this feeling of physical and mental balance attached to self-management. To perceive that other people, events, and circumstances, exert more control over our lives than we do personally results in anxiety and depression, which are detrimental to bother physical and mental health. Hence the need to look more inwards than outwards. Instead of focusing on people and events around you (which many times you lack control

over), it is best to look in the right direction-
You. That's the only factor you can change.

When you go through situations, understand
that there isn't much to what you can do about
what happened or how it transpired, but when
it comes to yourself, you can always choose and
decide. You can decide how you feel about what
happened; you can decide what next to do, you
can decide how you want the event to influence
you. Rather than play the victim (as is the norm
in our society today), you can choose to move
on and forget it ever happened. Suppose it was
a positive occurrence, to can also decide to
celebrate it instead of beating yourself over the
next possible negative occurrence. You can even
choose to express self-care. Whichever way,
know that self-management (or control) affords
you the opportunity of deciding whatever,
whenever.

Seeing that the feeling of self-management is
only normal, do not put up resistance each time
you experience that feeling. What you should
resist is the urge to 'let go' and put up blames.
In place of letting go, remind yourself of the
essence of self-control- your mental health,
physical health, an opportunity to decide a lot,
and ultimately, to achieve your goals. By
focusing on these, you are capacitated to
control more than you thought you could. So,
you have not only felt the need for control like

other humans do, but you have also channeled your need to control to a healthier region. Eventually, we all need to assume some control level as it isn't the only natural; it is also healthy.

Proactiveness

The principle of self-management is almost incomplete without proactiveness because to be proactive is to take control. Truly, life can put us in overwhelming and discomforting situations, but our reaction at such moments could also spur difficulty and inability to get better with our accomplishments. Do you respond reactively or proactively? To be reactive is to be in a state of no control. This is the case, as with people who are often found putting blames. The situation of things influences the attitude of reactive people, and if you agree, virtually every one of us has had a part in this reactive response. Your reactive response is what throws you in that condition of desiring to assume control. However, we channel this desire for control to the wrong channels.

Proactiveness is an essential characteristic of personal and professional success. It involves an objective evaluation of a situation, after which you take responsibility for deciding how things will then begin to turn out. To be proactive is to act before or in preparation for an occurrence. Inconsistency doesn't work in being proactive.

Except you are consistent with the practice of being proactive, you'll only record little progress. But by making certain choices and adjustments, you can be sure to record long-term success.

Healthy Lifestyle Choices

Sometimes, being proactive and taking back control of your life starts with making healthy lifestyle choices, learning to embrace self-care, identifying what excites you and sets you on course, or just something in that line. These choices are either taught or are outcomes of adjustment made to previous bad lifestyle habits. Let's see.

- **Get enough sleep**

  The need for enough rest and sleep cannot be overemphasized, and that is because the quality of our sleep affects our thinking and productivity. You really can't do much about self-leadership when you are exhausted. Self-leadership involves some level of alertness and consciousness. Hence, get enough rest. Sleep for as long as you feel relaxed and calm enough- at least for you to 8 hours (which is the recommended daily average sleep time). You might also want to try going to bed at the same time every night and waking up at the same time every morning. This helps the optimal functioning of the brain and much more, influences a good structure for your activities.

- **Maintain a healthy diet**

  It isn't just enough to get enough sleep; you should also maintain a healthy diet. Your diet has a level of impact on your health and productivity. As much as you can, ensure your diet contains fruits, green leafy vegetables, and lots of water. These will provide you with the essential nutrients needed for coordination, balance, and alertness of the mind and body. If you are one of such individuals who snack a lot, you might want to watch out for junk and unhealthy snacks. They are usually not the best for you.

- **Reduce alcohol and caffeine consumption**

  Although alcohol and caffeine are quite advantageous, people who consume them tend to do so extremely, thus being on the receiving end of the side effects of alcohol and caffeine. Excessive consumption of alcohol and caffeine can lead to anxiety, insomnia, and even a decreased coordination, all of which are dangerous, especially for someone who has decided to embark on the journey of self-leadership and self-growth for the greater good.

- **Give yourself a break**

Although taking control of your life involves a lot of planning and executing, no one lives life working, all day, every day. You can choose to look into your hobbies, take exercises in between, and spend time with nature, anything. Whichever way, just have fun. The truth is, unlike your childhood days, when everyone around you seemed indebted to you and always wanted to see you happy, things are really not the same now. This is adulthood when you have responsibilities. Funnily, these responsibilities include your happiness as an individual. So, engage in activities that make you happy. Take a walk, go shopping, take breaks, have fun, be happy. This sort of balance between work and recreation helps to stimulate your mental health.

- **Take some time off social media**

> True that. Social media can be draining. It has also been discovered to be time-consuming. With increasing conflicts and baseless arguments, social media appears to no longer be a platform for connecting people. Instead, it spurs comparison and false information, which are unhealthy. This isn't to demean social media, but as much as you can reduce the time spent there. That ample time can be divulged into something more productive. Also, ensure to sift the information you see on social media. While some of them are valid and helpful, others are merely false and bias; to do this is to be in control of what you need your mind with, and invariably, the attitude you put into the achievement of your dreams.

Still On The Journey To Taking Control

The reality is that the things we cannot control outweigh those we can exert control over, and in cases like this, making healthy lifestyle choices is not enough. Do we then dwell in the knowledge of our limit to assuming control? Not at all, because to dwell in that knowledge is to live within uncertainty, fear, and helplessness.

Regardless of the gravity of things beyond our control as humans, adopting certain tips (relative to the principle of self-management) is instrumental to the process of taking control. Doing this further allows you to live your best as the tips are fundamental to your thriving in a world filled with uncertainties. Let's see.

- **Define your values**

    Identifying your values affords you a structure for your pursuit. It helps you to set priorities and, in the long run, influences how you spend your time and resources. The values of an individual define their goals and influence their actions. In defining your values, you need to highlight those things that are of importance to you. You can then proceed to check if your skills and abilities are supportive of your values. If not, you can make plans on what to do, skills to acquire, people to meet, to further boost your confidence and identity with those values of yours. This is a better way of assuming control over your life as it spurs determination rather than living life scattered, aimless, and without purpose.

- **Declutter your space**

  An act as straightforward as decluttering can be what you need to further assume control over your life and the things that pertain to it. To declutter is to act based on your values. If you still harbor things and people who disagree with your values, you might just want to consider cutting them off. Declutter your physical and mental space and have some focus on yourself and your goals.

- **Build the right network**

  We will always have a thing or two to take from our close friends and associates, but not everyone is good for you. You wouldn't be good for everyone, either. Rather than waste your time making more friends and enlarging your circle, focus on building the right network. In building the right network, you focus on adding value to people knowing that sooner or later, they too can be in positions to render assistance- as little as cheering you up when you have a bad day. This might imply you are selective with your association, but it's okay. So long as it helps to channel you on the right course and brings you inches closer to your pursuit, by all means, be selective. Look out for those who have similar goals and values with you or, better yet, those who uphold yours and inspire you to do better. Building this type of social network helps to strengthen your will and pushes you till you reach the finish line.

- **Have a to-do list**

As you should already know, to-do lists enhance productivity. However, not everyone knows how to go about to-do lists to make the most of their time. The smart side to to-do lists is to keep it short. If you're going to have a to-do list for your daily life, there is really no point keeping a long list: the shorter the list, the more realistic the activities, and the better achievable, as well. Shortlists prompt you to want to do all you can to clear out the list, and that clearly depicts an ounce of control over what you do with your life, your time, and your resources. Identify the more important (and urgent) activities, and focus on clearing those ones first. As you get better with clearing your daily to-do lists, you realize the level of improvement doing that has helped you attain in your personal pursuit as well. No more will you get engrossed in the things that do not matter.

- **Set goals and make plans**

Goals are the bigger picture you envision. When you are clear on your goals, you avoid being caught up in things that do not matter. Setting goals help you to be more particular about your pursuit. It influences your focus. With your goals clearly stated, you are better able to identify potential hazards and, as such, work towards avoiding them. You can start by penning down each goal alongside steps to be taken towards achieving them. As you proceed to work on those goals, you might discover a need to modify or adjust some. Don't fret. It is only an indication of your growth. Remember, the focus is on you being in control. You can take any direction so long as attaining your goal remains the focus. Stop wishing, set goals, make plans, and execute them. That's control.

- **Keep learning**

  Like you already learned in an earlier chapter, learning is without limits. Embracing the art of learning is highly essential in the process of self-leadership. There is always a lot to learn. To learn is to build mental capacity and to approach life with a more open mind. In learning, you access new skills, ideas, and even people, all of which are instrumental to your personal growth and development. Asking questions is also an important process of learning that shouldn't be disregarded.

- **Learn to manage your emotions**

  Yet another thing to learn. Emotions are fantastic experiences but can be harmful when not controlled or properly managed. To maintain human relationships, which, more often than not, are the base for attaining goals, you'll have to learn to understand, interpret, and respond to your emotions. This will avoid a case of reacting based on your feelings.

Sometimes, you might need vents for your emotions. An act as simple as talking to someone can be all you need to assess your mood and get a hold of how you feel before proceeding to react. Sometimes, learning to manage your emotions aid your decision-making. Rather than making decisions when overwhelmed and under pressure, an understanding of how you feel and why you feel that way is a good way to cool off and deliberate before making decisions. Never act based on your emotions; it is harmful and unhealthy- to you, to the people around you, and to the goals ahead of you.

- **Be optimistic**

Negativity ruins. What more? It lowers esteem, hope, and confidence. For a person scheming to take control, you should endeavor to shun negativity in every way (in thoughts, in deeds, in words, and even from people). This is because there will be times that your results look nothing similar to your efforts. Your ability to remain positive regardless is what will keep you going at such times. If you observe closely, a good percentage of people who seem not to have control over their lives are quick to give up at the sight of difficulties. Know this, things don't run smoothly always, but with a positive and never give up attitude, you be sure to pull through, always.

- **Try new things**

  The upside to taking risks is the privilege of opportunities. You may never know how many opportunities you'll lose if you relent on making efforts and trying new things. Trying new things can further expand your interests and influence your adjustments to your values and, at the same time, to your goals. Identify your fears and face them boldly. It's step one to taking risks and trying something new.

Although life seems hard, difficult, challenging, and terrible even, the reality is that it is only a phase, and you are in control. Truly, it may appear that the odds aren't in your favor, know that the time will pass. As such, focus on the coming times, focus on what you can control.

When it comes to your life, yourself, space, and decisions, it is up to you to take the lead.

You don't have to wait till it gets so bad before you start thinking of taking some steps towards getting unstuck. You have to step up to take control of this situation that seems to control you. Sometimes, 'stepping up' might require you accepting the truth about some of the defects in your habit and also letting go of some things and people you still hold on to but are detrimental to your growth and development. Again, until you take a step to make it happen, nothing is ever going to happen. So, take the chance, make a change—this time, for the better.

While you are responsible for inculcating the habits and lifestyle choices earlier discussed, it is essential to note that you don't have to try them all at once. For you, it's a change, and chances are better implemented slowly, steadily, radically. At the end of the day, a shift in your mindset, your definition of possibilities, and lifestyle habits is what is needed in assuming control over your life.

SELF LOVE

The desire for a better or improved quality of life can be a reality if we cease to neglect "self." Several people give so much attention to the external world and leave their personal world in a state of anguish, pain, and void of love. Whatever you want to see, experience, and achieve is first conceived within; this is a significant pointer that you should revisit yourself and set things right. You deserve all the best in life, you are entitled to a better quality of life, and you can get these things when you regard yourself better; "**You have to love yourself**." Yeah, loving yourself is made easier when you understand the true concept of what love is.

What Is Love?

Love covers a scope of solid and positive emotional and mental states, from the great virtues or good habit, the most profound relational friendship, and the most effective pleasure. It is one of the most profound emotions we express as humans. Being free in nature, we experience nights flailing wildly, attempting to appreciate what it is and how to know whether we have it. How might you describe something so wild and adaptable?

That is the dangerous thing about love; we can feel it in a wide range of states—when we're cheerful, dismal, furious, confounded, or excited, and our mentalities about affection can go from affectionate love to fixation and pleasure. We even use love as an activity, as a power to keep our associations with partners, or loved ones and family, together.

- **Love is chemistry**: From a scientific perspective, love is a great and perpetual neurological condition. Love is science, and it's not something you can easily control. When you feel genuine love, the mind can deliver a set of chemicals that permit you to experience love in diverse expressions.

- **Love is infatuation**: This is a sense of dedication as an aspect of love, which could be a dedication to self or someone else. It is a state where you are helplessly devoted or dedicated to a course, self, an individual, and things.

- **Love is commitment:** This is interwoven with "love as an infatuation." It is the effort we put towards anything and anyone, as a result, constantly work to develop and nurture the persons, self, and things we have affections for.

What Is Self-Love?

There is a misconception that self-love is similar to having a big ego, which is never true. Now there lies the question, "what does self-love really mean?" Self-love is treating yourself with respect, having due regard for your happiness, well-being, and quality of life. It is not living less of what you deserve.

Self-love is a condition of gratefulness for oneself that develops from activities that help our physical, mental, and profound development. Cherishing yourself doesn't mean you believe you're the sharpest, generally gifted, and most lovely individual on the planet. All things considered, when you love yourself, you acknowledge your supposed shortcomings, value these alleged inadequacies as something that makes you who you are. At the point when you love yourself, you have compassion for yourself.

Self-love isn't about moment satisfaction. Another pair of shoes or eating a whole pizza may cause you to feel great at the time (or taste heavenly), yet the inclination isn't enduring and could be harmful over the long run. Self-love implies giving yourself what your body, mind, and soul require for life's journey. It isn't gratification, and it isn't pursuing a physical or passionate high. The act of self-love is simply the act of nourishing and supporting yourself.

Self-love can mean something different for every individual since we, as a whole, have various approaches to deal with ourselves. Sorting out what self-love is for you as an individual is a significant piece of your mental health.

The subject matter of self-love is vital and dynamic. For these reasons, a widespread definition of what self–love is to our individuality is outlined below.

- Self-love is trusting yourself.

- It is setting healthy boundaries.

- It is the ability to forgive yourself.

- Prioritizing yourself.

- Connecting to yourself.

- Being nice to yourself.

Where It Comes From?

More often than not, several people overlook or neglect the existence of self-love. By chance, they are brought to light about self-love, and they ask where it comes from? If truly I should love myself and it exists, is it then right inside of me?

Self-love is that game-changing energy that has been trapped inside of you for so long, and it's time to give it full expression. Take note of this: no matter how twisted the concept of self-love could be, it can only come from within **YOU.**

It's quite cool and intriguing to seek love from the outside, but the truth is the outside can only give you a fair measure of love. It is the love that you express from yourself to yourself that can remain and really stand the test of time. It's quality because it creates a healthy, stable environment and mental state, serving as a springboard to connecting with yourself, the environment, and people out there—in a general sense, improving the quality of life.

When it is said that self-love comes from **YOU,** this is what it means:

Self-love comes from the fact that you understand and agree that you are valuable and special. There can only be **YOU.** Remember that there is no other version of you out there; there is no upgrade of **YOU** out there. You are the only **YOU**; hence you are unique, valuable, and special. Self- love negates you belittling yourself, but not still launching you to a world of pride. Take a deep breath and reflect on these words; it is of great necessity because even if you experience love from the outside, there will be that emptiness right within **YOU** seeking for love within to fill it up.

Self-love births from constructively assessing yourself. The consciousness you have about yourself can go a long way to seeing yourself in a better picture, which in turn stirs up self-love. You assess yourself to get a better result out of you and not diminish your value or quality. Self-love is driven towards positive improvement and not towards a state where you downgrade yourself, lose self-worth, and end up with a deteriorated mental health. Don't be scared to assess yourself, but do so to the benefit of your self-development.

Self-love comes from creating a distance between things that makes you unhappy and yourself. It expresses when bad energy is put out. Finding a way to keep your happiness flowing is a source of a gushing flow of self-love. You cannot have self-love without being "happy with yourself." Appreciating your present state and having faith in a better version of your personal life to come is a good point to let the love flow. Everything and everybody that interacts with your life in one way or the other have their significance; what you have to do is to weigh them and set things right. No matter the significances, it shouldn't push your happiness away. Always being happy will result in self-love.

Self-love springs up from your ability to cushion the feeling of your inadequacies. The situation of feeling inadequate or having the view of your imperfections take over you has resulted in pathetic conditions in many lives. These conditions include; low self-value or esteem, little or no self-growth, decapitated mindset, life trauma, and several ugly occurrences. The good news is that self-love will go a long way in healing those situations; you just have to note your inadequacies, work on them for improvement, and not place them at the top of the table, causing harm to your well-being.

Self-love comes from you always seeing the bigger positive picture of yourself. What a life booster that is!! We all agree that life isn't constant, that we are bound to experience changes. The changing nature of life itself has created the need for us to change towards adapting and getting the better out of it. So, having a positive picture of yourself advancing towards these changes via the process of self-growth and development is just perfect.

Do You Love Yourself?

This is a relevant and crucial question that demands sincere answers. Several people have a misconception of self-love, hence miss out on loving themselves. Ask yourself right now the question, do I love myself? It may be difficult supplying the answer right now, but not to worry, stay calm and attentive as we go through this section, which will help you realize the answer to this question concerning yourself.

Let's be sincere. If you have to ask the question, there is a high probability that you know the answer. It could mean that you don't love yourself, or you don't love yourself completely.

A leading pointer that you don't love yourself is that you don't trust yourself, your abilities, and instinct. At the point when you don't have genuine self-love, you seek others for answers. While there's nothing amiss with requesting advice, and you get the advantage of alternate points of view, something fascinating occurs for you when you don't have self-love:

At the point when you are confronted with a choice—little or enormous—you "freeze." You think about it over for somewhat more than is most likely important. You consider your choices, yet you actually can't choose. You feel a flood of nervousness about what the correct action should be. Individuals instruct you to listen to your gut; however, you don't have the foggiest idea of how to do that. You don't have a clue whether the dreadful feeling you're encountering is an indication that you shouldn't settle on a specific choice—or if it's simply just a bump you need to get over.

When you don't have self-love, you become afraid of making a critical mistake. You feel this way since you don't trust in your capacity to deal with whatever comes your direction. This is the point at which you go to others to offer you the responses no one but you might have.

It is absolutely right to hold others of high esteem, but not to your own detriment. Irrespective of what their thoughts about you could be, the truth is that you know yourself better than everyone else. No matter what, always tell yourself that you are "first-class" and that you can always be better.

The action results in your shrinking, and you see yourself as small. If you think others are better than you, what do you stand to gain thinking this way?

You scarcely appear in a relationship or interaction with the outside world. Your default position is to limit your voice. You need to be as low-support and pleasant as could reasonably be expected, so you renounce yourself and hand over control to another person.

The absence of self-love has a well-known path. You will shrink or reduce yourself so much and adjust to what another person needs you to be

—so much that you awaken one day and have no clue about who you truly are. Now, you've regressed into an out and out misery or depression without a reasonable bearing throughout everyday life.

In addition to all that has been said, here is a checklist that would go a long way in determining if you love yourself. If you love yourself, most of the following will be evident in your life.

- You believe in yourself and have the mindset that you can achieve whatever you want.

- You harness your strengths and improve your weaknesses.

- Your intuitions or voices in your head tend to be positive and better than they use to be.

- You forgive yourself for all mistakes and climb up the ladder for a better version of yourself.

- You are firm in your decisions.

- You treat yourself right, put yourself first at appropriate times.

- You switch to positive thinking and view of life.

- You let your voice be heard.

- You stick to the right people, with the positive vibes, saying bye-bye to toxic relationships.

- You become a source of optimism for friends and family.

- You smile more and cry less.

- You go after fulfillment, making the best out of your time.

- Hold on to happiness, no matter the situation.

- You desire to learn more and improve the quality of your life and others.

- You see every day as an opportunity to do something amazing and worthwhile.

Importance of Self-Love

For some individuals, the idea of self-love is an exaggerated hypothesis, and they frequently disregard its importance. Individuals try to be perfect, and perfectionism is viewed as a more prominent resource than self-love. When we talk about self-love, it is easy to picture somebody reading self-improvement guides or embracing a tree; however, self-love is substantially more than that. Plenty of studies have demonstrated that self-love is the way to mental prosperity or well-being and keeps misery, anxiety, or depression under control.

The present world is patterned in such a way that we are kind of bound to contend with one another, or even ourselves continually. We are continually attempting to arrive at our transient objectives and attempting to better ourselves to meet up the expectations set upon us by society. We focus on the outward distraction so much that we forget to focus on the things that matter within ourselves. The fact is that the things we find within ourselves should matter more because they contribute to loving who we are. Neglecting this truth has resulted in how we wind up being excessively hard on ourselves very regularly without figuring it out. We all are pretty much snooty and devoured by our work, social communications, life objectives and goals, end of the week plans, etc.

Love is the main thing that keeps us going and makes us less automated in a world that expects us to work, think, and act like customized bots. Everybody needs love, and we burn through the majority of our effort on loving others — be it companions, life partners, children, or family. We as a whole prefer to spread the adoration, yet the inquiry is — do we produce enough for our own selves?

We can't generally hope to depend just on external sources for love, and that is where the idea of self-love comes in. An individual who practices self-love will never need to rely upon others to be happy, and it is an empowering feeling to be cheerful within.

The question is, **why should you love yourself?** Here is the summary; to grow, to advance, to extend what your identity is, and to at last arrive at a point where you can adore the godlikeness inside you. There are unique and game-changing qualities that you have but are yet to be discovered. You are the very first person that can dig out those qualities and abilities that lies within you. But you will need an interaction between self-love and self-confidence.

Here is how it works; self-love creates an awareness that you should trust yourself and your abilities. You then move to the next phase, where you now actually trust your abilities and yourself as a whole. This interaction is a sure game-changer that elevates you and switch you to the progressive side of life.

Follow through the following points, as they are all pointers to the importance of self-love.

- **It helps you make healthy choices:** At the point when you hold yourself in high regard, you're bound to pick things that support your well-being and work well for you. These things might be through eating healthy, exercising, or having a healthy relationship. You express your affection for yourself by doing things that help you to appear in life as the best version of you.

- **Ability to be successful at anything:** It has been experienced that an absence of self-love can crush somebody's profession and chances for progress. How many exceptionally fruitful individuals do you think looks in the mirror each day and say belittling and demeaning words to themselves? It is as straightforward as that. Without self-love, you definitely decline your capacity to be fruitful at anything. Failed businesses, relationships, thoughts all come from an absence of self-love.

- **Fills the gap left by external sources of love:** Nobody has a superior comprehension of your deepest thoughts, needs, or necessities than you do. In any event, when you attempt to share with others how you feel, they may identify and show sympathy; however, they'll never entirely experience life a similar way you do. The number of individuals who know you better than you realize yourself is likely thin if existent by any stretch of the imagination.

- **It grants you the gift of forgiveness:** Holding on to hard feelings can truly hold you down. When you love yourself, you see the ability to forgiving yourself as well as other people for things that previously occurred and consequently can't be controlled. You begin to take responsibility regarding your actions while releasing the load of blames you place on yourself for the mischief others have caused you. In doing such, you discharge the hold others have on you.

- **Helps boost your relationship with others:** At the point when you invest energy handling your feelings, you are burrowing somewhere within yourself and getting to the center of what your identity is. As you work to cherish and acknowledge yourself and be straightforward, you urge others to do likewise. This permits you to open up and associate with others on a more profound level, unafraid to show the pieces of yourself that are harsh around the edges and see the equivalent in others.

As days go by, it is becoming evident that self-love should be treated with all seriousness.

How Our Upbringing Can Affect Our Self-Compassion

When we talk about the effect of upbringing on self-love, we refer to the interaction of parenting, family, and the individual's childhood environment on the individual's ability to love his/herself.

Encounters you had when growing up, and maybe your present associations with relatives or family members, all affect your self-love. At the point when you were a child, you were exposed to all that occurred, and your mind was highly susceptible to impressions. You didn't have authority or control over a large portion of what you heard, saw, and experienced in your life.

Our self-love development is filled (to some degree) by the relational peculiarities or family dynamics we were educated in. It is an inheritance that leaves its imprint, and that is, in some cases, hard to heal. Particularly if it originated from a dad or a mother who never loved his or herself and who wasn't talented in taking care of our necessities, giving consolation, or showing at least a bit of kindness to heart.

The renowned social anthropologist Margaret Mead disclosed something essential to us. She keeps up that the family is that first social gathering where our interacting method figures out our identity (or possibly a decent piece of it). Our parents are the ones who have the obligation and commitment to fill our "tank" with sufficient supplements and rich parts. They ought to guarantee that there is no absence of security, love, and attention. They should provide crucial support and drive, which will assist us with strolling through this world to believe that we are valuable individuals.

The building of our self-love starts in childhood. Nonetheless, does this imply that our character is totally dictated by all that we encountered in childhood and early youth?

In mental issues, all that occurs in childhood has a major impact, yet it doesn't totally determine our identity. One thing we think about humans, and specifically the mind, is that our adaptability and capacity for improvement is huge. Nonetheless, regardless of this, we can't move away from the incredible significance of our upbringing. The nature of our interaction with the individuals who care for us is totally key. They don't just give us food, yet in addition to a passionate and educational legacy.

Here are experiences that could have led to a state void of self-love.

- **Being compared to others**: One of the most exceedingly terrible mistakes that a parent can make is to compare one kid with another. Whether the comparison was to a relation or even yourself when you were your youngster's age, your kid sees such comparisons as you saying they are sufficiently bad. No two individuals are actually alike, and no positive outcome originates from comparisons.

- **Controlled life**: Instead of organizing the entirety of kid's activities, they should be guided just until they obtain certain abilities. Young ones should be given space to investigate and find things independently. As they get more seasoned, it becomes easier to talk with them about making great decisions without causing it to appear as though you're pushing your own desire onto them.

- **Criticism**: When individuals face criticism in childhood, it becomes an awful experience. For example, a statement like "I am disappointed in you" can affect the individual's willingness to try new things and limit how he/ she sees his/herself.

- **Harsh and too high Standards**: Setting too high standards for an individual in childhood will be the opposite of the desired outcome. It creates a state where the individual fear is becoming a disappointment, which makes the individual suffer in the chains of fearfulness.

Other experiences that could lead to a life filled with self-love and self-affirmation.

- Being listened to.

- Being spoken to in a polite manner.

- Being surrounded by supports and encouragement.

- Being told that life isn't a bed of roses, that things can turn out sour, but victory is sure.

- Being valued; receiving attention and care.

Recollect your encounters now. You probably observe that experience regularly, however not generally, can be arranged as either positive or negative, and relying upon which they were, you developed self-love, or you are void of it. In any case, this feeling can extend into adulthood, prompting an assessment of yourself as being either a success or a disappointment.

If your case has been positive, hold on to the self-love you have. But if yours have seen the rough edges of life, there is still hope as your best option is to let go of those experiences and love yourself. You are unique and not a disappointment.

How Does Self-Love Relate To The Mindset And Thoughts About One's Self?

Following this book with unwavering attention, you will discover that it wasn't possible to do justice on the subject of self-love without considering the "mind." This is a bold claim that there is a relationship between the mindset and self-love. Alright, let's clearly decipher the relationship that exists between these two important life matters.

Let's have a quick relook or reflection on what mindset is all about.

The mindset is our belief or perception about ourselves, abilities, people, and life in general. It creates the mental world in which we live, a determiner of how or what picture of the life we see. It is very important because it is the control room of our consciousness and subconsciousness. Several mental health and self-development experts have held on to the notion that we have the "fixed mindset and the growth mindset."

- **A fixed mindset**: is a form of mindset where the individual's belief and perspective cannot be changed. This is the kind of mindset that prompts individuals to make an unhealthy statement such as "I can't be better" or "I will never fit in."

- **A growth mindset:** this is one with the belief in change, adaptation, and a better picture of everything. This kind of mindest prompts comments like "failure happens, but I can and will succeed."

Looking at self-love, we established that self-love is the condition where you value, nurture, trust, and forgive yourself, holding on to the possibility of a better you.

The question is, how do they relate? The simple answer is that self-love is a condition where you work or improve your mindset because you have realized that only you can be you and deserve a better quality of life.

Your thoughts are a product of your mindset, which shows forth in your daily actions or activities. If they are on a wrong scale, you begin to live out bad energy and end up in depression, pain, and failure. But if the reverse is the case, then you are on the positive side of life. Self-love is healing for your mindset and thoughts, which then results in productive activities and living.

Ways to Love Yourself

Much has been said on this subject matter, but it would be appalling if it all ends without taking appropriate actions. Let's get right into it, outlining ways you can love yourself.

Understand that you are very important

One lesson that you must learn is this: You are totally the most important individual in your whole universe. Your entire life is experienced through your eyes. Your associations with the world and everyone around you, your thoughts, and how you decipher events, relationships, activities, and words are all essential parts of your life. This shows that you are the main player in your world.

You may very well be someone else with regards to the amazing plan of things; however, with regards to your comprehension of the real world, you are the main important thing. What's more, hence, your world relies upon the measure of love and care you give to yourself.

For the exception of life situations that were brought on us before we were born, your relationship with yourself is the highest determinant in molding the sort of life routine you experience. The less you love yourself, hear yourself out, and get yourself, the more angry, confused, and frustrating your world will be.

Yet, when you start and keep on loving yourself more, the more all that you see, all that you do, and everybody you interact with begins to turn into somewhat better inside and out.

Take Responsibility

In case you're battling with self-love issues, will you assume responsibility for your circumstance?

I think taking responsibility is the most remarkable characteristic we can have throughout everyday life. Since actually, **YOU** are at last liable for all that occurs in your life, including for your happiness and unhappiness, victories and disappointments, and for the relationship you have with yourself.

Accepting the pain and moving forward

There could be memories that keep hunting you, making life so uncomfortable and filled with pain. Sometimes you alone really understand how hurting your past mistakes and experiences have been. It's understandable how agonizing it could be but remember that nobody is perfect, and you deserve to be free from the pain. Just as you have those horrible experiences or mistakes, there are several other people out there going through the same, but the pain has no right to drain your happiness and wellbeing.

A few of us mistake self-love for unending energy and optimism. Furthermore, we think this is the best activity; all things considered, shouldn't positive vibes just draw in more sure vibes? Yet, in all actuality, your endless optimism gets tried.

Since we, as a whole, have a dark side, we as a whole hold agony, contempt, and pain. Disregarding these real factors gobbles us up and drives us to collapse profoundly and mentally.

Permit yourself to be straightforward with what your identity is. Forgive yourself for your past deeds, those things you are embarrassed about, and keep moving to that better picture that always exists.

Find and open your heart

It's time you reconcile with your cold and unopened heart. Make this one inquiry of yourself: do you completely love yourself?

Tolerating your blemishes and your flaws would one say one is a thing, however adoring an individual who can have your thoughts, your feelings, your indecencies, and your slip-ups? That is a totally more elevated level of self-love.

Find your life story. Follow your way from youth to the individual you are currently.

Understand yourself in the most personal manner conceivable, and discover the purpose behind each negative feeling, each shameful demonstration, and each word and deed that you presently wish you never uttered and carried out.

Remove the skeletons from your storeroom and attempt to recall why they are there in any case.

Maybe the main thing you will find is that most pieces of our character have a reason, and those that don't can be learned away.

Possibly you have bogus understandings of the real world, or injury, or sentiments of victimhood.

Possibly you see the world uniquely in contrast to what it really is, and therefore, you did things you presently know to not be right.

Discover the causes and follow your past. Figure out how to love yourself such that no one but you can. Don't allow yourself to be embarrassed by yourself about your past and begin to understand it.

When you conceal past feelings, you basically put yourself in a cage made by yourself.

The main way out is to push through the awkward facts you've been subduing. If you go close to the edge of the cage, you feel great distress. In that spot of distress, you can at last deal with past injury and agony.

Care is the way to escape from your emotional enclosure.

The more you manage past feelings through care, the less emotional disturbance can happen.

Emotional disturbance depends on something that transpired sometime in the past, something you haven't let go of.

Through care, you can let go, and afterward, you can be free.

Figure out what you want to do with your life and act

Become a friend to the word purpose. Discovering your purpose and acting towards it can make you happy and add meaning to your life. Your purpose takes away your attention from negative vibes and places it on the course of achieving something great. Get busy with yourself, and achieve all goals you ever dreamt of.

Surround yourself with people with positivity

This is an important aspect several people overlook. We're totally impacted by who we invest the vast majority of our time and energy with. Think about this statement from Tim Ferriss:

"You are the average of the five individuals you invest the most time with."

Valid, right?

So on the off chance that you believe that a portion of your companions are harmful and have a propensity for putting you down, you should locate some new ones. You know, individuals you really like and respect.

On the off chance that your companions are positive and inspiring, you'll start thinking better about yourself too.

CHANGE

Here we are, in a world characteristic of several systems. The interaction between these systems and the human mind and body has resulted in our desires, purposes, fulfillment, and sense of well-being. The world systems are dynamic in nature, which means they are subject to change. The propensity to change has also rubbed on us, such that our desires and state of mind are not constant. For us to embrace this flow on a positive scale, we also should be ready for change and adapt to the best state possible.

Change simply means to stop doing things the way you use to and embrace a new method. It is becoming a different and possibly a better person. Several things in our personal world need to be changed to have a better interaction with the external world at large, which are our thoughts, beliefs, and even our appearance (this could help spice up things a bit).

Change Your Initial Thoughts

Are you in a state of depression? Or it could be that you find yourself making the wrong moves and choices; hence you are deprived of the sweet spice of life. Deteriorating mental health may have been your present situation, and self-confidence may be long gone. But do you believe that it can all be better? This is where you begin to experience a turnaround because all these situations have a root in your thoughts. Switch your thoughts to the positive. You may be thinking, "What's the connection." Alright, let's go a full stretch and see things clearly.

There is a connection between our thoughts, feelings, and actions. The interaction of these three elements results in the different states or results we experience daily. This is more drawn to the widely known concept termed Cognitive Behavioural Therapy (CBT).

It's accepted that the more we see how every last one of the three components influences us, the more control we can have over our responses. Actually, CBT broadly draws these segments as a triangle, showing how we think influences how we feel, how we feel influences how we behave, how others act influences how we think, etc.

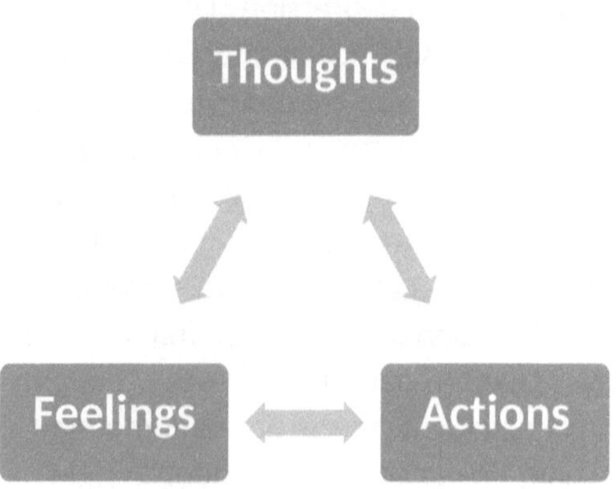

Let's have some real-life scenarios. As individuals, one of our most basic instinctive assumptions is that an outer activity legitimately educates how we feel. For instance, you neglect to react to a message that I sent you six days earlier, and I feel hurt by it. Or, on the other hand, your kid gets back home with one more "awful day" report, and you feel down. Or on the other hand, your life partner neglects to finish the tasks you requested that the person in question does on many occasions, and you feel furious and exasperated. CBT would reveal to us that it is the thought(s) that we have about those circumstances, not simply the circumstances that are causing those feelings. For instance, when you don't answer my message, an instant thought of, "I'm not that essential to you," comes up in my mind prompting me to feel hurt. It's my flaw he can't carry on now "When your companion doesn't do what you asked, possibly you think, "For what reason am I the one in particular that actually does anything around here?" This all results in appalling behaviors and decision making, which could end up hurting your mental health.

Alright, so since you have a little more knowledge of the relationship between your thoughts, feelings, and behavior and how they interface, you are likely considering some solution for it. While the CBT trio of thoughts/feelings/actions would propose that every one of these elements is similarly significant and similarly fit for influencing all the others (and I would concur), the best spot to begin to make a change is with our thoughts. Why? They are the helm of the connection. What's more, (here's the enormous takeaway!) if we can change our thoughts, at that point, we can change our feelings or emotions and our actions. On the off chance that we can enable our young ones to change their thoughts, we can help them better manage their feelings and actions.

One approach to do this is to be more mindful of the psychological stunts our brain plays on us, also called cognitive distortion. As the name would propose, cognitive distortions are thoughts in which the matter's truth is twisted or covered up somewhat. It is essential to have the option to recognize and challenge twisted thoughts when they happen to acquire a more neutral and balanced perspective and consequently decrease reactive feelings and conduct. Check out these practical approaches; on the off chance that I imagine that I'm not essential to you; I will feel hurt. In any case, if I'm ready to supplant that idea with a more positive one, for example, "I realize that my companion has been truly stressed this week and I realize that our friendship is valuable to her, then she's presumably not reacting right now since she's having too much work on her hands," I will feel significantly better. Additionally, on the off chance that I imagine that my life partner does nothing around the house, I can challenge that idea (and forestall a tense situation) by thinking, "really, he/she did a great deal with the children this week. It's baffling that they neglected to do what I solicited, yet there were plenty of different things that they completed."

Negativity

We have said a lot so far; all that the previous paragraphs are trying to do is take out the clouds of negativity, which are the results of you not being able to challenge your thoughts. Negativity could have been a result of childhood experiences and also the cognitive distortions we talked about.

Get realistic in your thinking; life gives us all a fair share of opportunities. "You are great," "You can be better," your situations don't define you, but you define yourself. Challenge every unhealthy thought, stay far away from assumptions, and just keep seeing a brighter side of life.

Your Confidence Can Bring Change

Everybody respects a self-confident individual. We may even begrudge them a bit! Self-confident individuals appear calm with themselves and their work. They welcome trust and motivate trust in others. These are appealing attributes.

It's not in every case simple to be confident in yourself, especially in case you're normally self-critical or if others put you down.

Self-confidence understands that you trust in your own judgment and capacities and that you esteem yourself and feel commendable, paying little attention to any flaws or of what others may think about you. It is trusting in your qualities, which is important to your mental well-being.

The following is what you see in a self-confident person

- Always optimistic.

- Admits mistakes and learn from them.

- He goes for what is right, even if there are several oppositions.

- Willing to take risks.

An absence of self-confidence will have a telling effect on your behaviors, which could even lead to self-destruct and an unstable mental state. Self-confidence helps clear out the clouds of negativity and enrich you with the desired energy to move on with life. Self-confidence takes you out of the state of worrying that you aren't good enough and launches you into a realm of better performance in different areas of your life.

Here are ways to build up your self-confidence and experience change on a positive scale.

Stop comparing yourself to others

Whether you compare what you look like with your social media or compare your earnings with others, it isn't a healthy practice. Truth be told, a recent report distributed in Personality and Individual Differences found an immediate connection between envy and how you feel about yourself.

The research found that individuals who compared themselves with others encountered envy. What's more, the more jealousy they encountered, the more regrettable they felt about themselves. It very well may be an endless loop.

Focus on times when you think about your riches, assets, accomplishments, and traits. Imagining that others are better or have more will dissolve your trust in yourself. When you notice you are drawing comparisons, advise yourself that doing so isn't useful. Everybody is running their own race, and life isn't a competition.

Pay attention to your body

It's difficult to like yourself when you're mishandling your body. Holding back on rest, eating an unhealthy diet, and ceasing from exercise will negatively affect your well-being. Studies reliably show that physical activity helps confidence. You could hit the gym or get a workout instructor and aim to be healthier overall, which will result in more self-confidence.

Practice self-love

Self-love includes treating yourself with graciousness when you commit an error, fall flat, or experience a mishap. Addressing yourself cruelly won't propel you to improve. Truth be told, studies show it will, in general, have the contrary impact.

Instead of beating yourself up or calling yourself names, make a move at addressing yourself as you'd converse with a trusted friend. Cut yourself a little leeway, laugh at yourself, and advise yourself that nobody is void of errors.

Challenge the negative thoughts

It is not strange that in different instances, the thought of "I will fail," "it won't work out," and other related thoughts keep coming to mind. They may or will come, but it is left for you to either accept or discard them. Always challenge negative thoughts because they never mean well for you. Bear this in mind that whatever thought that comes or whatever situation that is present, there is always a better version around waiting for your embrace.

Always remember all you have achieved

It's anything but difficult to lose confidence if you hold on to the notion that you haven't accomplished anything. Make a rundown of the apparent multitude of things you're glad for in your life, regardless of whether it's getting a decent score on a test or figuring out how to be great with that hobby of yours. Keep the rundown close by and add to it at whatever point you accomplish something you're pleased with. At the point when you're low in confidence, pull out the rundown, and use it to help yourself to remember all the awesome stuff you've done.

Your Looks Can Help Your Confidence

Looks aren't everything, but they sure do help our confidence. Do a quick recall of the above section, where the ways of building your confidence were outlined. We call recall that one of the ways vividly explained is that we should take care of our bodies. Very true.

Several individuals have been stuck in their shells because they don't have an appealing body shape. Why suffer such setback when there is a straightforward solution, which is "Start working out."

"If you look good, you feel good." This is one true fact we all can't dismiss, as we have experienced such at one point in life. Check out how a six-year-old kid has been properly taken care of and dressed. You begin to see how elegant he or she walks. The kid does this because the confidence has been escalated, and they feel on top of the world that very moment. It even goes to the extent where the kid wants his/herself to be checked by everybody. The morale is top-notch.

Regular exercise and workouts play a crucial role in balanced mental health and confidence. You may not be in terms of this theory, but keep calm and follow through with this great revealing aspect of this piece.

You definitely realize that exercise is useful for your body. Yet, did you realize it can likewise support your state of mind, improve your sleep, and assist you with managing depression, nervousness, stress, and that's only the tip of the iceberg?

There are numerous benefits of exercise or working out, one of them being a lift in confidence. Working out can cause you to feel more good with yourself and boosts your self-confidence. As per heaps of research, physical activity is straightforwardly and by implication related to confidence.

One of the most straightforward ways exercise can support your confidence is by making you look better; however, conditioning muscles and getting more fit are only the start. There are endless ways physical activity can help your confidence.

Check out loads of benefits to your mental health and confidence when working out.

Treats depression

Studies show that exercise is effective on gentle to moderate depression as viably as antidepressant medication—yet without the side-effects, obviously. As one model, research done by the Harvard T.H. Chan School of Public Health found that running for 15 minutes every day or strolling for an hour cuts down the danger of significant depression by 26%.

Exercise is an effective pacifier for depression for diverse reasons. Above all, it advances a wide range of changes in the brain, including neural development, diminished inflammation, and new activity patterns that boosts feelings of calm and well-being. It additionally releases endorphins, incredible synthetic compounds in your brain that stimulate your spirits and cause you to feel great. Finally, exercise can likewise fill in as an interruption, permitting you to locate some quiet time to break out of the pattern of negative thoughts that feed depression.

Helps out with anxiety

Exercise is a characteristic and viable enemy of anxiety, hence used in anti-anxiety treatment. It reduces pressure and stress, helps physical and mental energy, and improves well-being through the arrival of endorphins.

Attempt to see the impression of your feet hitting the ground, for instance, or the mood of your breathing, or the feeling of the breeze on your skin. By adding this care component—truly zeroing in on your body and how it feels as you work out—you'll improve your physical condition faster. Yet, you may likewise have the option to intrude on the progression of steady worries going through your mind.

Decreases Stress

We all agree that our body never feels good when under stress, right? Your muscles might be tense, particularly in your face, neck, and shoulders, leaving you with back or neck pain or agonizing head pains. You may feel a contraction in your chest, a beating heartbeat, or muscle cramps. You may likewise encounter issues, for example, a sleeping disorder, heartburn, stomach ache, running stomach, or regular pee. The concern and distress of all these symptoms can prompt more stress, making an endless loop between your brain and body.

Working out is a viable method to break this cycle. Just as delivering endorphins to the mind, physical activity assists with loosening up the muscles and calm pressure in the body. Since the body and mind are so firmly connected, when your body feels good in this way, your brain also feels the same.

Good therapy for Attention Deficit Hyperactivity Disorder (ADHD)

ADHD is a mental disorder that results in an above-normal level of hyperactivity and impulsive behavior. This is an issue where an individual could have a problem paying attention to things or even sitting still for a long time.

Having regular exercise or working out consistently is one of the least demanding and best approaches to decrease the manifestations of ADHD and improve concentration, motivation, memory, and mood. Physical activity quickly supports the brain's dopamine, norepinephrine, and serotonin levels—all of which influence attention and focus. Along these lines, exercise works similarly to ADHD drugs, for example, Ritalin and Adderall.

Helps out with trauma

Proof proposes that by truly focusing on your body and how it feels as you work out, you can really enable your sensory system to become "unstuck" and start to move out of the immobilization stress reaction that describes trauma. Rather than permitting your mind to hover around, give close consideration to the actual sensations in your joints and muscles, even your inner parts, as your body moves. Activities that include cross movement and that engage with the two arms and legs, for example, strolling (particularly in sand), running, swimming, weight practice, or dancing—is a portion of your most ideal decisions.

Open-air exercises like climbing, cruising, mountain biking, rock ascending, whitewater boating, and skiing (downhill and cross-country) have additionally been appeared to diminish the symptoms of trauma.

Keeps the body in shape

Some of the time, self-confidence issues are attached to body discernment. Regular exercise helps gain confidence by improving our body shape. While working out, you're probably going to fortify and tone your body, and seeing these outcomes can incredibly improve your confidence and assist you with better feelings on the way you look.

Being in shape includes having a very much conditioned body and a better stance – all angles associated with self-confidence. When an individual feels good about his/herself, it's simpler to make friends, and more associations in life imply more confidence.

Boost productivity

Perhaps the ideal approach to clear the brain is to exercise consistently. Exercise allows you to start all over again. Moreover, if you propel yourself exercising, you can understand new possibilities, and this thus helps self-confidences. Frequently, what you thought was a significant issue before working out vanishes after.

You feel stronger

Standard exercise makes your body stronger and takes down the danger of hypertension and chronic diseases. It additionally assists in controlling weight and lessen stress, depression, and uneasiness. At the point when you have physical strength, you frequently increase mental quality.

Increased brainpower

Exercise makes you more astute. At the point when you do a high-impact workout, you feed your brain with important supplements and oxygen, improving intellectual capacity. After exercise, you will, in general, feel more engaged and ready to finish the undertakings of the day all the more proficiently along these lines improving your confidence.

During an endurance workout, a molecule called irisin is delivered to the mind through a chain response. Researchers trust it has neuroprotective impacts and can initiate genes associated with memory and learning. Through analyses on mice, specialists of Harvard Medical School and the Dana-Farber Cancer Institute found that irisin and FNDC5 become raised in the brain during endurance work out.

Feelings of control and achievements

By and large, exercising has countless advantages to well-being and the brain that we can't resist having a feeling of control and achievement. Working out takes work, devotion, duty, and care for oneself, which encourages gigantic feelings of confidence.

CRITICAL THINKING

Everybody thinks; it is our make-up to do as such. In any case, a lot of our thinking, left to itself, is one-sided, contorted, partial, ignorant, or downright biased. However, the quality of life relies in many ways on the nature of our thoughts. Disgraceful reasoning is expensive, both in cash and in quality of life. Quality thought, notwithstanding, must be efficiently developed.

Critical thinking is the capacity to think plainly and reasonably, understanding the logical association between thoughts. Critical thinking has been the subject of much discussion and thought since the time of early Greek scholars.

Critical thinking may be depicted as the capacity to take part in intelligent and independent reasoning.

In a general sense, Critical thinking involves your ability to reason. It is tied in with being a functioning learner as opposed to a detached beneficiary of information data.

Critical thinkers thoroughly question thoughts and presumptions instead of tolerating them at face value. They will consistently try to decide if the thoughts, contentions, and discoveries reflect the whole picture and are available to find that they don't.

Critical thinkers will recognize, investigate, and take care of issues efficiently instead of instinct or intuition.

A critical thinker will:

- Understand the connection between ideas or thoughts.

- Establish or identify the essence of the idea.

- Identifies faulty thoughts.

- Handles problem in a systematic way.

- Thinks receptively inside elective frameworks of thought, recognizing and evaluating, as need be, their suspicions, suggestions, and practical consequence; and discusses adequately with others in sorting out answers for complex issues.

Being Critical In Your Thinking

A quick fall back on what critical thinking is: Critical thinking is the capacity to think plainly and reasonably, understanding the logical association between thoughts. Critical thinking may be depicted as the capacity to take part in intelligent and independent reasoning.

In a general sense, Critical thinking involves your ability to reason. It is tied in with being a functioning learner as opposed to a detached beneficiary of information data.

Unfortunately, not everyone falls into the category of a critical thinker since many just accept and jump to conclusions on whatever information they get from the outside world or their minds.

How do I become critical in my thinking? This is one question running through the minds of many at different times. Now, let's get right into the mix of transforming you into a critical thinker, hence creating a positive shift in your life dealings.

Being critical in your thinking involves the following key steps:

- **Knowledge**: For each issue, clear vision puts us on the correct way to solving it. This step involves identifying the contention or the issue that needs solving. Inquiries ought to be made to get a profound comprehension of the issue. Now and again, there is no real issue, accordingly, no compelling reason to push ahead with different strides in the basic reasoning model. The inquiries in this stage should be open-minded to permit the opportunity to talk about and investigate principal reasons. At this stage, two principle questions should be tended to: What is the issue? What's more, for what reason do we have to settle it?

- **Comprehension**: When the issue is identified, the following stage is to comprehend or understand the circumstance and the realities lined up with it. The information is gathered about the issue utilizing any of the research strategies that can be embraced, relying upon the issue, the information accessible, and the cut-off time needed to tackle it.

- **Application**: This stage follows the previous one to finish the comprehension or understanding of various realities and assets needed to take care of the issue by building a linkage between the information and relevant resource needed for action. Mind guides can be utilized to investigate the circumstance, construct a connection between it and the core issue, and decide the ideal approach to push ahead.

- **Analyze**: When the data is gathered and linkages are established between the primary issues, the circumstance is analyzed to determine the solid points, the weak points, and the difficulties confronted while taking care of the problem. The needs are set for the fundamental causes and decide how they can be tended to in the solution. One of the usually utilized tools that can be conveyed to analyze the issue and the conditions around it is the cause-effect chart, which partitions the issue or problem from its causes and means to recognize the various causes and arrange them dependent on their sort and effect on the issue.

- **Synthesis**: At this stage, when the issue is thoroughly analyzed and all factors considered, our choices are shaped by the way we handle issues and the underlying courses to follow to transform this choice into action. On the off chance that there are many solutions, they ought to be assessed and organized to locate the best solution. One of the devices that contribute to picking the problem's solution is the SWOT analysis that will, in general, distinguish the solution's strengths, weaknesses, opportunities, and threats.

- **Take action**: The last step is to assess the problem that can be put into action. The result of critical thinking ought to be transferred into action. On the off chance that the choice includes a particular project or team, a strategy could be actualized to guarantee that the solution is embraced and executed as arranged.

The critical thinking strategy can be embraced to supplant feelings and scrutiny inclinations when attempting to think about a circumstance or an issue. The ideal time for embracing critical thinking fluctuates dependent on the issue; it might take a few moments to some days. The benefit of adopting critical thinking is that it adds to extending our points of view about circumstances and expanding our reasoning prospects. In any case, these means should be converted into a strategy that guarantees that the concluded goal is all-around accomplished and incorporated between all the included bodies.

When to be critical

We have established who a critical thinker is and how to embrace the method of critical thinking. It would seem as if we should think all the time critically.

Although critical thinking is consistently valuable and can be applied all over, in a practical sense, it's not useful to think this way constantly. It's not only about where you apply critical thinking but also when you apply it.

A straightforward guideline to decide if you should utilize critical thinking in a given circumstance is the point at which the consequence of a problem, activity, objective, or situation (a head-scratcher) is Substantial. At the end of the day, utilize critical thinking when the result has a critical effect on your individual circumstance or business.

The Reasons/Importance of Critical Thinking

Critical thinking here and critical thinking there!! What the heck is going on? The voices acknowledging the concept of critical thinking gets louder, then there must be reasons for this. Several people, write-ups, and life coaches keep singing critical thinking praises; then, it must be somewhat important. Well, it's time we see things for ourselves. What are the reasons for critical thinking? See the answers below:

- **Critical thinking is universal:** Critical thinking is a general thinking skill or aptitude. I don't get this' meaning? It implies that regardless of what way you take, the calling you seek after, the profession you pursue, and even basic life situations, these abilities will consistently be pertinent and will consistently be valuable to your prosperity. They are not explicit in any field.

- **Improves communication skills**: To best communicate, we have to realize how to think plainly and methodically — which means the practice of critical thinking! Critical thinking likewise implies realizing how to break-down writings, thus, improve our capacity to grasp.

- **Help in self-reflection**: Without critical thinking, how might we truly carry on with a meaningful life? We need critical thinking to self-reflect and assess our lifestyles, feelings, and opinions. Critical thinking furnishes us with the apparatuses to assess ourselves in the manner that we have to.

- **Promotes creativity**: By practicing critical thinking, we are permitting ourselves not only to take care of issues but also to think of new and innovative plans or ideas to do so. Critical thinking permits us to dissect these thoughts and change them in like manner.

Let's have a quick look at the outstanding benefits of critical thinking.

- **Better decision making**: There's no uncertainty about it — critical thinkers settle on the ideal decisions. Critical thinking helps us manage everyday problems that come our way, and at times this manner of thinking is done subconsciously. It causes us to think freely and trust our instincts.

- **Help form a well-informed opinion**: There is no deficiency of information coming at us from all points. Also, that is actually why we have to utilize our critical thinking abilities and choose for ourselves what to accept. Critical thinking permits us to guarantee that our conclusions and opinions depend on current realities and assist us with figuring out such additional clamor.

- **Improves relationships**: While you might be persuaded that being a critical thinker will undoubtedly cause you relationship issues, this truly couldn't be less obvious! Being a critical thinker can permit you to all the more likely to comprehend or understand the viewpoint of others and can assist you with getting more liberal towards various perspectives.

- **Boost career success**: Critical thinking is pivotal for several career paths. There has been a misconception that critical thinking is useful to scientists or researchers alone, however legal counselors, doctors, journalists, architects, bookkeepers, and analysts (among numerous others) all need to utilize critical thinking in their positions.

  Truth be told, as indicated by the World Economic Forum, critical thinking is one of the best abilities to have in the labor force, as it breaks down data, consider new ideas, take care of issues with creative solutions, and plan efficiently.

Many errors we have been prone to overtime can be a thing of the past with critical thinking skills. It's an encompassing concept that touches diverse areas of life to solve problems.

What Brought About Your Negative Thinking?

Every individual on the face of the earth has negative thoughts at different moments in a whole day. Nonetheless, our lives' energy and positivity are being controlled by the reality of how we are managing these negative thoughts. Regardless of whether you overlook them or acknowledge them, it is all up to your will. On the off chance that you won't evade these negative and unwelcoming thoughts, at that point, these negative thoughts can drag you down, and even they can suck the life and positive vibes out of you. We may have numerous negative thoughts during our time since we are humans. Be that as it may, it is essential to consider how to dodge them in an ideal manner.

First thing first, can you identify what negative thinking is? No need to worry. Let's look at what counts as negative thinking before we can actually decipher what brought them about.

In case you're somebody who breaks down your thoughts, it may be difficult to separate negative thoughts from the normal worries that everybody has. Feeling pitiful or sad about a displeasing event is typical, similarly as stressing over financial itches or relationship challenges is something we as a whole do now and again. It's the point at which those emotions become constant or repetitive that it results in negative vibes.

Here is a definition: Negative thinking is a psychological mentality of envisioning or anticipating the absolute worst results on circumstances, events, and situations. The mind can deliver thoughts that are not positive for what the individual needs. At whatever point a trying situation emerges, an individual with negative thinking pre-empts a negative result before it has even happened or being followed upon.

Now, let's fall back to the question, "**What brought about your negative thinking.**"

Several reasons can cause negative thinking. Research has shown that negative thoughts can be a symptom of a bad mental health condition such as generalized anxiety disorder (GAD) and obsessive-compulsive disorder (OCD). But let's hit on primary sources that could be responsible for your negative thinking, which will be unraveled by moments in your lifetime, that is, the past, present, and future.

- **Shame in your past**

Several things may have happened in the past, which you aren't proud of. It could be your mistakes or the cruel and demeaning environment where you were brought up. Get this right; we do things that we are humiliated about. We do things that don't turn out how we figured they would. The disgrace of those past errors or disappointments can rise every now and then. At the point when they do, we can flounder in them like a pig in the mud, or we can recognize that they occurred and refuse to let them drag us down. Everybody commits errors, and nobody is that perfect.

So how do you fix this?

The ideal approach to dealing with mistakes is to learn from them. Take a look at what you did, and afterward, ask yourself what you might have improved in that circumstance. When you have your answer, at that point, put your past behind you. It is no more. You can't change the past, but you can learn from it. Try not to whip yourself for committing an error except if you have neglected to learn from that mistake. Do you continue committing a similar error again and again? What would you be able to do to break that pattern of conduct? Perhaps keep away from places or individuals that are associated with you committing that error over and over. Dodge practices that lead to the mistake in any case. Assume back responsibility for your present by learning from your past as opposed to binding yourself to it. Whenever you have broken the chains to your past by learning from your mistakes, you can seek after your future and make the most of your present.

- **Anxiety about your present**

Anxiety about the present is reasonable. Many of us stress what individuals consider about us, regardless of whether we're working admirably grinding away and what the traffic will resemble on our way home. Negative thinkers frequently think of the direst outcome imaginable: that nobody in the workplace likes us, our manager is going to reveal to us we've accomplished awful work, and the traffic will make us late to get the children. Once more, this comes from the fear of losing control.

Worry is an augmentation of fear, fear that we are overlooking something significant. We are so over-burden with information, a lot of it is unnecessary that we struggle to recall the things that are really important to us. The fear of overlooking something significant joined with day by day updates on the information on individuals committing those uncommon yet calamitous errors due to overlooking eat into our minds.

So how do you fix this?

The most straightforward path is with organization and schedule. Make a daily plan for the day. Make an ace daily plan for the family so that everyone recognizes what should be done and who needs to do it. Dispose of the anxiety by assuming back responsibility for your day by day life. Try not to feel that you need to do everything yourself and assign a few things to the family's remainder. If we are, for the most part working together, at that point, the heap is a lot lighter for everybody.

- **Fear of the future**

Individuals normally fear the unknown and the mysterious. Individuals have attempted to anticipate the future for all of human existence, from taking a look at broken turtle shells to noticing the trips of winged creatures to tossing sticks or bones on the ground. Individuals fear the future and what it may bring. Will it bring fortune? Or then again, catastrophe? Science has gotten very great at foreseeing results in the present moment inside a shut framework like elections or the climate. However, the normal individual truly worries over the future and invests a ton of energy pondering what will occur in the short and long haul for them.

Numerous individuals attempt to keep up an inspirational attitude toward the future and imagine that they will succeed or accomplish some objective they have set for themselves if they simply continue attempting. Others are tormented by thoughts and fears of disappointment and catastrophe. We burn through so much time and energy agonizing over things that haven't occurred at this point and may never occur. We are paying interest on a charge card we haven't utilized at this point.

So how do you fix this?

Fear of things to come originates from an apparent absence of control about your future. Probably the ideal approach to retake control is to make an arrangement for what's to come. A bit by bit guide for where you need to be one month from now, one year from now, or one decade from now. No arrangement endures contact with an adversary, and our foe is the fear of things to come. Yet, a plan gives us some proportion of power over our life. We know where we need to be and pretty much the means we have to take to arrive—layout little, reachable, and momentary objectives that will prompt a bigger, more mind-boggling long-haul objective. A plan will help lessen the fear of things to come, and by expansion, decrease the number of negative thoughts that spring up every once in a while.

How It (Negative Thinking) Hurts You

When we become involved with a portion of the hard times in our lives, there's a propensity to let negative reasoning overwhelm your brain. Troublesome or difficult circumstances will, in general, make the psychological combination expected to transform even a positive individual into a wellspring of pessimism. At the point when we flounder in self-pity or have an awful perspective on life, the issue essentially gets intensified the more we consider how bad everything is.

We frequently hear that we are what we eat, but on the other hand, we're what we think. If you think negatively constantly, that is everything you'll draw in into your life. You could be a regularly enthusiastic, happy individual, yet when you yield to pessimism, you gradually slide down into being a spout of negative energy for the individuals around you.

Negativity has been noticed to have an all the more effect that we understand, nonetheless. Having negativity in your considerations and your brain, or having a negative perspective on the world can influence your body. Being a Negative person is burdening on the brain and body. It's normal for individuals who are reliably negative to be consistently sick or sickly, with cold or just for the most part, ill-feeling.

Negative reasoning generally corresponds with raised pressure or elevated stress. Elevated stress is attached to lack of sleep, raised pulse, hypertension, dietary problems, drug use, liquor misuse, memory issues, upheavals of outrage, nervousness, or quite a few other conceivably genuine medical problems. As it were, you can think of yourself debilitated. Negative perspectives also influence the brain's synthetic substances and upset the hormone balance in our bodies, causing us to feel messed up.

If you've ended up in a consistent descending twist of negativity or sentiment of sadness about things, it's an ideal opportunity to run after changing your point of view. It's probably influenced your well-being here and there already, if you understand it or not, and the more you take to roll out an improvement, the greater that impact will be.

By assuming responsibility and deciding to take a look at things from a positive viewpoint for a change, you're giving yourself traction that you need to escape the propensity for negativity. It can require some investment to eliminate a pessimism mien; however, with patience, things' bright side has a kind of effect when you see it.

In summary, negativity would result in the following

- Anxiety.

- Depression.

- Mood disorders.

- High blood pressure.

- Inability to make progress and achievements in life.

- Self-criticism.

- Irrational fears.

How Negative Thinking Can Hold You Back From Accomplishments

As negative thoughts are dashing through your head, it's difficult to focus on doing something else, particularly your goals and aspirations.

Your goals can appear to be difficult to accomplish when you're in the wrong perspective. You may even conclude that it's not justified, despite any potential benefits, to begin a project or pursue your goals since you're encountering all these negative thoughts that state you can't do it.

There are basic laws that guide one on the path of success for whatever endeavor or goal to be achieved. Let's highlight them quickly:

- **Law of belief**: You become what you believe. If you accept that you will fail at something, at that point, you assuredly will. On the off chance that you accept that you will succeed, at that point, you have won a large portion of the fight. You simply need to proceed to get it done. Negative thinking will always place you on the wrong belief. With negativity, you will end up saying, "I can't succeed at my goals."

- **Law of cause and effect**: For each move that you make, there is a relating response. On the off chance that you are not content with the outcome, it depends on you to work in reverse and change the earlier activity that prodded it. Negativity will spur you to make the wrong moves and choices, resulting in bad results.

- **Law of control**: At the point when you like yourself and how you are running after the objectives that you have set, at that point, you will feel that you are in full control of your life. You are in the driver's seat, and you give orders. A negative thinker is never in control of his/her life.

- **Law of expectation**: What you expect becomes a great drive. Do you expect that you will get the outcomes you need? At that point, you will have more confidence that it will work out. Unfortunately, confidence and motivation cannot thrive in the presence of negativity.

- **Law of attraction**: Your prevailing thoughts act like a magnet that will draw individuals, thoughts, and conditions. On the off chance that you need to draw in positive things, at that point, you likewise need to think positively. Negative thoughts will only attract negative things, and people tend to avoid negative energy, hence making achieving goals impossible.

- **Law of correspondence**: Your external and inward world is in a state of harmony with one another. So you need to introduce yourself as a success in the world? At that point, start from within by making yourself look like a success. An individual wallowing in a pool of negativity will not see himself/herself as a success and, in the end, can't present himself/herself as a success to the outer world.

- **Law of mental equivalency**: You have your positive thoughts and assertions. Apply the standard of reiteration until it turns into your reality. At the point when you make the mental equivalent to what you want, that point, everything else will become alright. The issue lies with a negative thought, which cannot result in the positive affirmation needed.

Negative thinking disagrees with the school of thought of success, as outlined above. A negative thinker will find it hard to achieve life goals because he/she will end up doing the following:

- **Overgeneralization**: This is thinking something will consistently happen just because it happened once. On the off chance that a desirable task goes to another person once, you can't resist the urge to think, "Simply my luck! I miss out on everything."

- **Mental filter**: You select a solitary negative detail and stick to it. You may get bunches of positive remarks about your work, yet if one partner says something somewhat critical, you fixate on it for quite a long time.

- **Diving into conclusion**: Deciphering things negatively without facts to help your decision is a sign of this attitude. Regardless, you anticipate things will turn out for the worst. Before a critical gathering, for instance, you may let yourself know, "I'm truly going to blow it."

- **Personalization and blame**: This psychological twisting causes stress when you consider yourself liable for an event that isn't totally heavily influenced by you. For example, when you've hit a hindrance with a colleague, you think, "This is all my flaw," rather than attempting to pinpoint the reason for the issue so you and your coworker can get back on the same page. Then, it's likewise basic to put the blame of what you're going through on other people and markdown the manners in which you may be adding to the issue.

- **Discounting the positive**: It's a regular practice for you to make light of positive encounters by disclosing to yourself they don't count. On the off chance that you work superbly, you reason that any other person in your group might have done similarly also, so what does it by any chance make a difference?

Did any of those idea patterns sound accurate for you? It's an ideal opportunity to retrain your mindset so you can beat these nonsensical thoughts. Whenever you end up falling into these pointless idea patterns, you can apply the strategies underneath.

- **Remind yourself that your negative thoughts are not reality**: Negative thoughts attempt to fool you into believing that you'll never succeed. This isn't accurate. Imagining these thoughts and afterward discovering approaches to turn them around is critical. By utilizing methodologies, for example, this one, you will find that achieving your objectives isn't as hard or insane as it appears.

- **Analyze the evidence**: Don't just accept that your negative idea is valid. For instance, if you continue figuring your boss won't care for your thoughts regardless, review when she or your group hovered behind you in acceptance, even in the littlest ways. Try not to be reluctant to prove yourself wrong.

- **Use words or affirmations to force your mind to think the right way**: Did you realize that your mind will follow your words? Attempt it at the present time. Whatever you begin talking about will quickly assume responsibility for your thoughts. What about utilizing this for your potential benefit?

  Plunk down and list the principal areas you battle within your mind. Do you need more confidence? It is safe to say that you are continually demolishing things by your outrage? Do you generally think negatively? Do you trust you don't have the stuff to succeed?

  Write out "statements of a positive belief" for those pain points and keep them with you. At that point, discuss them again and again for the day—even murmur them in case you're around others.

- **Try meditation**: DON'T do it to get away from the world but meditate to prepare yourself to INVADE the world, and that is how you ought to meditate.

  The issue is that our minds and brains have headed out in a different direction, and we haven't reliably focused and prepared them. One of the best approaches to do that is meditation. On the off chance that you can figure out how to control your thoughts for only 10 minutes, you'll be better ready to control them for the day.

  For at any rate 10 minutes three times each day, stop and reflect—ideally when you awaken, have lunch, and before you head to sleep.

Positive vs. Negative thoughts

The efficacy and importance of positive thoughts can't be denied, even though occasionally it can appear to be similar to a cliché when you hear individuals discussing it. Well, irrespective of whether it is a cliché or not, the psychological and physical advantages of reasoning positively are a sure method to give you more confidence, improve your self-value, give you inspiration or motivation, and by and large sets you feeling better. Considering in any event, one positive idea consistently can have critical benefits for you.

Some logical investigations even recommend that thinking positively can diminish the probability of medical issues, similar to misery or depression, hypertension, and an assortment of different stress-related issues.

This sounds astonishing, yet what does it truly mean to think positively?

Positive thinking isn't just tied in with finding your inward smile. Numerous individuals infrequently have what they would consider happy inward thoughts; however, that doesn't mean they can't be content with themselves and their life.

Positive thinking (considering positive thoughts consistently) is more about finding the positive symbolism or imagery in your life and review things through more idealistic and optimistic views, particularly on the off chance that you have yourself into a trench of seeing things on the negative scale.

The most concerning issue with positive thoughts is that they wear off rapidly, and things like rejection, negative encounters, misfortunes, and heartbreak can, in no time, place you into a descending twisting that gets you back into that negative funk you detest.

Also, let's face it, being in a negative funk is a certain approach to strip your inspiration and leave you incapable of performing at the levels you realize you can.

All in all, how would you keep yourself positive in a world that appears dead set on cutting you down? Indeed, with the correct daily schedule of good thoughts, you can guarantee that you awaken each day feeling inspired and anticipating all that life needs to toss at you.

Here are a few hints so you can begin thinking positive thoughts consistently.

- **Be grateful for every morning you wake up to see**: Not to begin on a horrible note, but rather you woke up today. A few people didn't. Try not to consider it is as a heartbreaking ethical quality story; simply use it to recollect that you've won the best blessing life has to bring to the table – you're alive.

  It's so natural to dwell on the negative parts of our lives, yet we generally appear to miss the most obvious positive thing we have – life itself. Take a full breath, look outside your window, and wonder about your general surroundings.

- **Do not give into comparison**: I know, I know. It's anything but difficult to state, "Don't compare yourself and any other person." But by the day's end, we as a whole have desirous thoughts when we see someone we see to be more fruitful than we are. Be that as it may, consider it, are they truly better than you, and regardless of whether they are, does it by any chance make a difference? By investing energy being jealous, you are squandering energy on negative thoughts that could be spent seeking after something that gives you happiness.

- **Don't listen to haters**: There's no uncertainty that a few people are truly cowardly people who will very much want to destroy your day. All things considered, you should have it in mind that they can't if you don't give them a chance.

Overlook the haters. Excuse their bile for what it is − offensive remarks of unfulfilled individuals. Advise yourself that you are above them, and nothing they state will cut you down.

- **You just have to try, take a chance**: It's anything but difficult to avoid high risk and high reward out of fear of being named a failure.

  Have you ever seen that doing so really aggravates your feelings than if you'd recently faced the challenge in any case? We realize that rejection feels awful, and disappointment can weigh vigorously, yet lament or regret is a far more grounded feeling after some time.

  Try not to stop for a second if you get the opportunity. Let it all out and reveal to yourself that on the off chance that you come up short, it's not a problem. At least you attempted.

- **Accept that things end**: Indeed, even the best things in life all have an end, so don't stress over them. Try not to worry about how the great times and experiences will stop; simply appreciate them while they last. When they do at the long last end, be happy and grateful in the knowledge that something different that is good is on the way.

- **Focus on the good things in life, no matter how small they may be**: You will hit impediments during the day. Things don't happen perfectly all the time. The clue is that when you experience a challenge, don't dwell on it and decide to cling to the positives you can locate regardless of how little they may appear.

On the off chance that you find yourself in a traffic jam, don't worry about how it is slowing you down. Take inspiration in the way that you have an additional chance to tune in to the radio broadcast you have pleasure in. If you head to your nearby store and it's out of the spices you require for your evening party, purchase something different and make an alternate food magnum opus.

Focusing on beneficial things is an extraordinary method to increase the positive energy in your life. The enormous intensity of good energy is that even a progression of minute things can aggregate to huge outcomes – with positive energy.

All through the book, a lot of points have been hammered upon concerning negative thoughts. What we can boldly claim is that irrespective of the reason behind the negative thoughts, there is always a better option, which is never giving the thoughts a chance to blossom.

MAKING FINANCIAL DECISIONS

There is no doubt that one important aspect of our lives is our finances. We all clamor on the need for a better quality of life, a life void of pain, negativity, and a deteriorating mental state. One truth is a large percentage of our worries, pain, and fears are connected to the state of our finances. The need to balance things up urges us to venture into different career paths that demand success, which the success is a function of our actions, and on the same scale, our actions are functions of our thoughts, beliefs, or perspective. All these points to how essential this subject matter is to our mindset, and in general, the pursuit of self-growth or development.

Although problems may never stop occurring, humans should try everything possible to limit the sources of our problems. Following this book right from the first section up to this stage, you will discover that the problems we face daily result from the state of our mind, actions, and external environment.

One thing that troubles our mind's state is the need for survival and a sense of fulfillment. By default, in life's operation, our finances have a role to play in helping our quest for survival and fulfillment. There are many things we want to do, lots of places we want to go, several things we want for ourselves, and many of these desires can be met with funds. In a case like this, if there are no funds, there is definitely a problem, which will have a toll on the state of our mind.

Once you can't meet up with the bills, you start thinking, and at that point, a whole lot of negative vibe could get into the mix. This is just to let us know that in our quest for an improved life, our finances have a part to play, and it also depends on our mindset in making the right financial decision to alleviate the related problem on the ground. This section is straight the point piece to establish a better channel for making financial decisions to boost the quality of life.

Choices You Make With Your Money

We all desire wealth; in fact, human nature has an affinity for an atmosphere of abundance, where all we want is at our beck and call. The truth is our peace, sense of fulfillment, or even a better state of mind doesn't just depend on money, but on the choices, we make with the money we have, either little or numerous. The choices we make concerning our money and even other areas of our lives are enclosed in just two units, either positive or negative.

Examples of negative choices

- **Making large, unnecessary purchases:** A great deal of credit card debt comes from purchasing things you don't generally need. From that great apparel deal to eating out each day, those little transactions can pile up before long, and before you know it, you are left with a pretty loaded credit card balance.

  Evade this regret by advising yourself that credit is really debt, and the accessible balance on your credit card isn't genuine cash! It's cash you are borrowing and will have to pay back. If you presently have debt, quit utilizing your credit card and build up a debt repayment plan. Those store cards, credit cards, and vehicle loans can be appealing, luring you with discounts and insignificant interest rates. In any case, when things begin to add up and those initial rates vanish, your debt can turn into a bad dream.

- **Not Investing:** A truly awful choice is choosing not to invest your cash by any stretch of the imagination. If you think you must be a specialist in the stock market to invest, reconsider! There are a lot of options, and with innovation, contributing has never been simpler.

You can either decide to put your money into the stock exchange market, real estate, or business - whichever course you pick, or on the off chance that you choose to go with each of the three, it is important that you do your research and understands the rudiments of what you are placing your cash into. The stock exchange market can seem like betting or a major startling spot; however, not on the off chance that you understand what you are doing and have investment goals. The profits on the stock exchange average about 8% over the long run and are among the most mainstream types of investing out there.

- **Not saving a percentage of your income**: We fall in the mix up where all of our incomes goes straight into expenses or even incurred debts. This is understandable, and life at times may be more challenging, but not trying all possible best to save a little of your income doesn't sound good. No matter

how little it may be, saving $1 for a year
will turn out to be $365. Try, even little.

Examples of positive choices

When we talk about the positive choices we make with our money, we are simply referring to a counter approach to all the negative choices listed above. If you want to make the right financial choices, go through the list above and avoid those wrong choices outlined.

The Principle Of Saving

We live in a consumer-driven period in which we are inspired and rewarded for going spending our money. While we may appreciate the delights, services, and esteem of having the option to pay for decent things, we regularly fail to remember how these fulfillments trouble our pockets toward the month's end and in the long haul.

To cite a quote from a genuine legend, Thomas Jefferson stated: "Never spend your money before you have it." This is, in all probability, the best cash sparing or saving tip any of the extraordinary men in history might have imparted to us. On a fundamental level, it is conceivable to be accountable for your money matters as long as you comprehend three key standards to be specific: planning or budgeting, discipline, and essentially spending less.

Budgeting

Saving money begins with understanding what's going on with your money. Truly, the goal is to save, yet it should be all around organized and measured. Just when you set up the sources of your money, really, at that time, you have an extensive perspective on what's going on with your cash. It likewise gives you clarity and sets your desires regarding what amount you can essentially save throughout some defined time frame. There is no reason for being capricious, thus missing the mark concerning the desires. Understand the various sources, sum, and timing of where the cash is coming from and where it is going. Ensure you make arrangements for unexpected costs that appear from thin air.

If you are married, the spending plan ought to be made together to guarantee there is an aggregate purchase to arrive at the target as a family. Agreement of the two parts of a partnership is imperative to save money.

Whenever you have made an image of where your cash goes in a typical month, at that point, you can distinguish the patterns and trouble areas.

Discipline

In the wake of understanding your capability to save, you have to put aside the amount of the money you want to save as though you are taking care of a bill. Open an investment account or start a programmed saver plan and train yourself to store the sum each and every month. Since you must choose to cover your month to month bills, your savings funds sum must be dealt with similarly. All the more significantly, the reserve funds ought to be deposited at the beginning of the month before you even get an opportunity to spend it. You will see that your cash has developed, similar to wizardry, over the long run.

Spend less

As basic as it sounds, it is the most conventional yet viable approach to save. You basically can't spend more than you earn. By spending additionally utilizing some sources of borrowed cash, you are really spending more on paying interest. This borrowing amasses rapidly, and before you realize, you have gathered more debts than you can oversee. It's then an excruciating activity for a significant period just to dispose of it. Here are a few ways you can cut down on your expenses.

CONCLUSION

Every Individual is made up of the elements of thoughts, feelings, desires, and even instincts. All these elements simply operate in our minds. A shift of any of the mentioned elements to the negative will directly affect mental state or health. The interaction of these elements has resulted in our identification of self-worth, the pursuit of comfort, satisfaction, and fulfillment. For a reason, this subject matter is crucial to every individual. This book has shown the right path and approach to mindset, perspective, reality, self-control, self-love, change, critical thinking, and even making financial decisions; all of these aim to improve our mental state in general, our quality of life.